The
PENN STATE
FOOTBALL
Button
Book

The PENN STATE FOOTBALL Button Book

Martin Ford and
Russell Ford

TRIUMPH
BOOKS
CHICAGO

Library of Congress Cataloging-in-Publication Data

Ford, Martin, 1954–
    The Penn State Football button book / Martin Ford and Russell Ford.
        p. cm.
    ISBN 1-57243-571-2
        1. Pennsylvania State University–Football–History. 2. Penn State Nittany Lions (Football team)–Collectibles. 3. Penn State Nittany Lions (Football team)–History.   I. Ford, Russell, 1951– II. Title.

GV958.P46F67 2004
796.332'63'09748–dc22

                                                                                                              2004047898

This book is available in quantity at special discounts for your group or organization. For further information, contact:
    Triumph Books
    601 South LaSalle Street
    Suite 500
    Chicago, Illinois 60605
    (312) 939-3330
    Fax (312) 663-3557

Printed in Canada
ISBN 1-57243-571-2
Jacket and interior design by Patricia Frey
Button photos courtesy of Brian Spurlock.
Nittany Lion mascot photos courtesy of Steve Tessler/Mountain View Studios.

We dedicate this book to our mom and dad, Carol and Don Ford, who brought us up to be Penn State Proud; to our brothers, Doug and Cam, who joined us in backyard football games in which many great Penn State football moments were replayed with less skill, but just as much enthusiasm; to our Penn State alumni wives, Sheri and Barb, who fear that because of this book, they will now be known as the spouses of "those Penn State button nuts"; to our children—Jason and Kevin, who provided inspiration, and Jen, Josh, Lisa, Zack, and Jordan (the "real" Nittany Lion), who continue the Penn State tradition.

And to Mimi Barash Coppersmith Fredman, the "Mother Button Maker."

Contents

PREFACE

You Can Pin the Button Idea on Me

The goal back in 1972 was to make the name of a new bank–Central Counties Bank–a household word. What we did was make a 2¼-inch, simple, round, metal button a Penn State household item. And the process was anything but simple.

After the merger of Lock Haven Trust Company and the First National Bank of State College in 1971, they turned to Barash Advertising, a growing agency run by my late first husband, Sy, and me. Our challenge was to create a brand and an image for this new Central Counties Bank. As luck would have it, a dynamic young football coach named Joe Paterno was transforming Penn State football into a regional and national phenomenon. You could see the growing wave of support for Paterno and Nittany Lion football. We should cozy up to Penn State athletics, was our thinking. Tapping into that fervor seemed like the appropriate and easy answer to a complex question.

Tying Central Counties Bank in with Penn State sports had the potential to be a win-win proposition. But believe me, it wasn't a concept to bank on. No one, to our knowledge, had ever tried to do that. Luckily for all of us, the new president of the bank,

Elmer Grant, saw the idea's potential. He encouraged me to pursue it with their marketing director, Buck Snare. Initially, he wasn't very big on the button idea, so the original plan in 1972 had Central Counties supplying buttons for home games only, with no mention of the bank on the button. The first order was for only 500 buttons per game.

Those plans didn't last long. "Get the Goat" for the Navy game and "Hammer the Hawkeyes" for Iowa (a Big Ten foe before its time!) were so successful as the first two buttons that Elmer ordered more buttons with the bank's logo printed on them. Because the initial order for the year had already been placed without Central Counties on the buttons, two buttons–one with the bank's logo, another without it–were available for the Syracuse contest ("Crush the Orange").

The Nittany Lions started the 1972 season with a loss, and then reeled off 10 straight wins. They were on a roll, and so were the buttons. The Sugar Bowl matchup meant a special button and one of my all-time favorite slogans: "I'd Sooner Be a Nittany Lion." We liked it so much that we tied in the campaign with our sister billboard company, Morgan Signs.

Billboards all over Central Pennsylvania and New Orleans hyped the Sooner slogan.

When we first undertook the button campaign with Central Counties, Barash Advertising came up with the slogans. Then, thinking that a contest to select the slogans would add pizzazz to the buttons' overall effectiveness, the selection process alternated between a public contest and a private one for bank employees. Back then, the award for a winning slogan included a U.S. Savings Bond or free tickets to a Penn State game. Barash organized the campaign and helped with the entries.

In the early years, a small group of folks at Penn State—most notably Penn State sports promotion director Fran Fisher and Paterno himself—picked the winning slogans. Eventually, associate athletic director L. Budd Thalman became the primary Penn State point person. To their credit, Paterno and his colleagues insisted on good sportsmanship, as well as good humor, as the primary criteria for winning entries.

Obviously, the bank knew it had a winner on its lapel. To its credit, the sponsoring bank has always given away the buttons for free, to customers and noncustomers alike. For decades, the sponsoring bank has shipped free sets of buttons to anyone who calls or writes. The buttons did what they were intended to do—they tied in Central Counties Bank and their successor sponsors, Mellon and now Citizens Bank, with the community and Penn State.

In 1984 the bank and our firm parted ways. At that time, they were our largest client. That hurt. But losing our ties with the button hurt even more. For me, it was a sense of ownership—it was our idea, and we deserved to continue to service it. Alas, coordinating the project—the slogans, the manufacturing, the timely and accurate shipping to multiple locations—was too much for the new vendor. So, after a one-year hiatus, the buttons were back home. Never too proud to retrieve what originally was the result of our creativity, I accepted the return of the prodigal bank button with a smile on my face. Interestingly, the button program survived mergers with Mellon and with Citizens, a real testimonial to the value and quality of the promotion.

Whenever I am asked what I believe is the best promotion we have ever developed in our 45 years in this business, I respond without hesitation that it's the Citizens Bank button campaign. For an individual promotion to stand the test of time for nearly 35 years is beyond one's wildest expectations. The Penn State football button is whimsical and witty; low-cost and laughable; clever and collectible; healthy and historical; awesome and affordable; spirited and special; and good for town and gown.

Perhaps the most unusual thing that can be said about the button promotion is that two Happy Valley born and bred brothers would believe that a book written about it could sell! For me, that's reason to pop my buttons!

—Mimi Barash Coppersmith Fredman

ACKNOWLEDGMENTS

Inspiration for this book came from the enthusiasm of two brothers for their university and Joe Paterno's storied football program. We are proud to have contributed to the legacy of Penn State football through this book, and we hope that our readers will join us in the satisfying knowledge that by buying this book we are all giving back to Penn State. Specifically, a portion of this book's revenues will go to benefit the newly established "Back the Lions Raise the Roar Endowment," a university-administered fund intended to enrich and aid in the development and growth of the Penn State Blue Band, cheerleaders, and dance team.

We are truly thankful to everyone who made this book possible. Besides the very important people to whom this book is dedicated, we could not have written this book without the help and support of many others. So give a big Penn State thank-you to:

- Citizens Bank, current button sponsor, with special appreciation to Citizens Bank of Pennsylvania Chairman and CEO Stephen Steinour, Pennsylvania Western Region President Ralph Papa, and Pamela Crawley and Sylvia Bronner of the Citizens' Public Affairs office.

- Mellon Financial Corporation (former button sponsor), and to all of the Mellon employees who helped make this Penn State button promotion a success.

- Central Counties Bank, which merged with Mellon in 1984, because the buttons never would have started without CCB's then-president Elmer Grant's support of Mimi Fredman's football booster button idea back in 1972.

- Penn State University, including encouraging words from president Graham Spanier, coach Joe Paterno, and athletic director Tim Curley, as well as advice and help from trademark licensing manager Derek Lochbaum and assistant director of development–athletics Michelle Davidson (thanks Derek and Michelle for the Nittany Lion!). Also thanks to Penn State Sports Museum director (and author of *The Penn State Football*

Encyclopedia) Lou Prato, who gave us insight on publishing a book.

■ Triumph Books, our publisher, and particularly to founder and president Mitchell Rogatz and editorial director Tom Bast, whose enthusiasm for our book project and patience in its creation was critical. Thanks for sticking with us.

■ Barash Advertising, from whence the button idea was first born, and especially to senior vice president Mike Poorman. Mike, your PSU football knowledge is second only to Joe's, and gaining your friendship was as important as the help you gave.

■ The Collegiate Licensing Company representing the Fiesta Bowl, particularly Malinda Childress, for giving permission to use the button for our No. 1 ranked game.

■ Brian Spurlock, who took photos of the nearly 400 buttons contained in this book!

■ Steve Tessler, Mountainview Studios in State College, for the great photo shoot of the Nittany Lion with that particularly awesome Penn State student as the Lion!

■ The Nittany Lion Nation, among which are some very enthusiastic fellow football button collectors. It has been fun getting to know all of you. Special thanks to Hob and Betts Moyer and to Linda and Chuck Glidden, who with some understandable nervousness, very graciously let us borrow a couple of very rare buttons so that you would be able to see them all.

INTRODUCTION

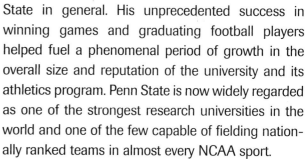

Part I: Origins

In 1966 the Penn State administration made a couple of pretty good personnel moves involving a pair of visionary 39-year-olds. They appointed our father, Donald Ford, as dean of the new College of Human Development so that he could pursue his "grand experiment" in multidisciplinary research and education. They also promoted Rip Engle's prodigy, Joe Paterno, from assistant to head football coach, where he initiated his own "grand experiment" emphasizing the importance of football players being true student-athletes.

Our father was dean for 11 years—a long time for a dean. He retired from Penn State in 1995 to write books, travel, spend more time with our mother, Carol, and do all those other things people look forward to doing in retirement. By comparison, Paterno has been head coach for 38 years—a *really* long time for a football coach. No one knows when he will retire. After a dismal 3–9 season in 2003, some are thinking "the sooner the better." But those who are more familiar with the history of Penn State football have reason to believe that Paterno is about to add another amazing chapter to his coaching legacy.

Over the years, Joe Paterno and his grand experiment got a lot of people hooked on Penn State football and Penn State in general. His unprecedented success in winning games and graduating football players helped fuel a phenomenal period of growth in the overall size and reputation of the university and its athletics program. Penn State is now widely regarded as one of the strongest research universities in the world and one of the few capable of fielding nationally ranked teams in almost every NCAA sport.

It is difficult to fully appreciate how special Joe Paterno's accomplishments are without citing some statistics. He has achieved athletic excellence with 20 top 10 finishes, 69 First Team All-Americans, and more than 300 wins at the same school (the only Division I-A coach to ever reach this standard). He achieved this excellence while also maintaining academic integrity, as evidenced by his 124 Academic All-Big Ten selections (the most of any Big Ten team since 1993) and by his team having one of the highest student-athlete graduation rates of any university in the country. To top it all off, he and his wife, Sue, have donated more than $4 million in gifts to support Penn State's academic mission and have helped raise even larger sums through their dedicated service as ambassadors for the university.

It is interesting to note that Paterno's "grand experiment" began in the context of growing social turmoil on college campuses throughout America. Student unrest related to Vietnam, women's rights, and the civil rights movement came to Penn State with much the same intensity as visited upon the rest of the country, and like so many other institutions, Penn State found it necessary to question some long-standing policies and practices. For instance, it is amazing to think that until 1968 female students were not allowed to visit men's dorms, or that in 1969 African-American students represented only about 3 percent of the entire student body.

Those were the same years that Joe Paterno produced his first two undefeated football teams while simultaneously emphasizing teamwork, high academic standards, and personal responsibility in his student-athletes. This example resonated well with the university's efforts to adjust to social change and conflict in positive ways.

It is easy to forget that while this was a time when "the whole world was watching," it was also a time of tremendous excitement and anticipation. Paterno's inclination to be progressive and to "think big" about the potential of Penn State football and Penn State University provided a positive counterpoint that was consistent with the growing aspirations of the surrounding community. Like Penn State, the State College area was on the move. For example, from 1967 to 1972 the State College Arts Festival was initiated, the Nittany Mall opened for business, the town's first high-rise apartments were built, and the newly constructed Centre Community Hospital began accepting patients.

In addition, to the retrospective delight of thousands of Penn Staters, in 1971 the Lock Haven Trust Company and the First National Bank of State College merged to form Central Counties Bank. This was a significant event for Nittany Lions fans because, as we now know, that merger and the need to promote the new bank gave birth to an idea created by Mimi Fredman and her State College-based Barash Advertising Group. The idea: promote the new bank by associating it with Penn State and coach Paterno's philosophy of pride and excellence by manufacturing and distributing free booster buttons for Penn State fans to wear and collect as they cheered on their team each week.

The football buttons fit quite comfortably with coach Paterno's belief that football should be fun. He encouraged players to enjoy the process of preparing for and engaging in a great challenge, with winning being the natural consequence of passionately investing yourself in something you love to do rather than the reason for making that investment. Consistent with this philosophy, the button tradition was a unique way to add a little fun to the Penn State football experience.

And what a tradition it has become! From its simple beginning in 1972 when the buttons were made only for home games (and for the 1972 Sugar Bowl against Oklahoma), the bank and its successors—Mellon Bank beginning in 1984, and now Citizens Bank since the middle of 2001—have continued to produce these buttons for every Penn State football game (and a few other noteworthy occasions) right up to today. That's 386 buttons (plus 11 variations) from 1972 through 2003, with no end in sight! In fact, the button promotion has grown symbolically far beyond its original purpose. The special legacy that Mimi Fredman, Barash Advertising, and the bank sponsors have given us in these buttons now connects us in pride, loyalty, and memory to Happy Valley, a great university, a fantastic football program, and a legendary coach.

We grew up in State College (actually in Lemont at the base of beloved Mount Nittany) and were Penn State students in the late sixties and early seventies. We remember seriously the tumult of those times, but we also remember fondly the fun

we had watching Penn State become a football powerhouse. Our attachment to Penn State football and the university came naturally as children of a Penn State professor and administrator. We began attending football games in 1964, and it was a big deal because our parents let us sit all by ourselves in those great wooden bleachers in the south end zone. Back then, you could not get much closer to Penn State football than that, and we loved it. For us and our two brothers, it was preordained that

Joe Paterno as Penn State's associate football coach in 1965, the year before he took the reins he has now held for 38 years. *Photo courtesy of AP/Wide World Photos.*

we would go to Penn State, and we did not mind the idea one bit.

When we became Penn State students, our brothers (Doug and Cam) were able to join the Penn State Blue Band (playing the clarinet and trumpet, respectively). But since our chosen instruments (piano and guitar) didn't work too well in a marching band, we searched for other ways to be a part of the excitement surrounding the football team. We were intrigued with the buttons and began to collect them, and we submitted slogans when the bank periodically would have public contests. ("Burn Wake Forest" was the Ford family's first winning slogan in 1974.) Sometimes our slogans were too cute ("Cheese Puffs" for Wisconsin) or a bit *too* clever ("Loose Nits Sink Zips" for Akron), but quite a few made it through the selection process over the years, including several of our all-time favorites: "No Santa Here, Virginia"; "Driving Mich Crazy"; "Champaign, You're Toast"; and "Kick Wisconsin's Dairy Air." In fact, after 32 years and 386 slogans, we can proudly say that 39, or about 10 percent of all those slogans, have been authored by our family.

Members of our three-generation Penn State family have supported our effort and our father's parallel effort to collect the Penn State football buttons, and many have contributed slogans regularly. A particularly notable early contribution was sister-in-law Pam's creation of a Nittany Lion banner designed to hold hundreds of buttons, which our parents unfurl at each home game from their tailgating perch. Our wives, Sheri and Barb, deserve special mention for being so tolerant of our somewhat unusual hobby. In addition to our parents' button collection efforts, Sheri's parents—Bob Coughlin, a retired Penn State administrator, and his wife, Betty—were tremendously helpful in acquiring buttons over the years. Barb's parents, retired emeritus faculty members George and Helen Guthrie, have also been supportive, as have Martin and Sheri's two sons, Kevin and Jason. Last but certainly not least, Russ and Barb's five children—Jen, Josh, Lisa, Zack, and Jordan—have had a significant collective impact as well as a particularly special interest since all are Penn State students or alums.

In sum, we feel "Penn State Proud" to be a contributing part of the Paterno legacy through our family's authorship of football button slogans and collection of these small symbols of one of the greatest sports programs of all time. While it may seem odd to some to make this connection, being proud of our rather unusual association with the Paterno legacy is exactly what motivated us to write this book. *The Penn State Football Button Book* is both a celebration of the Paterno legacy as well as our attempt to provide, for the first time ever, the complete, definitive, and self-proclaimed "official" collection of bank-sponsored Penn State football buttons.

In the next section we examine the Paterno brand of football excellence in more detail. In a word, Penn State football is about *cycles*. There is the cycle of seasons (with its new complement of buttons) that brings us back each fall to see if the glorious triumphs of past years can be repeated. Then there is the cycle of players that brings renewed excitement and hope as they mature from high school recruits to notable young players on the depth chart to team leaders. Finally, there are cycles of excellence in the level of accomplishment that each team attains as professor Paterno and his fellow educators work to facilitate the maturation process from year to year.

In an effort to understand this cyclical pattern, we have carefully studied the characteristics that the greatest Nittany Lion teams seem to have in common. This analysis has enhanced our understanding of the Paterno coaching philosophy and our appreciation of the special nature of his coaching accomplishments. In the end, it is this understanding that leads us to make the following bold prediction: coach Paterno and his Nittany Lions are on their way to another national championship run beginning in 2004 and culminating in 2005. Read on, and you will understand why.

Part II: Cycles of Excellence

Anyone who follows Penn State football knows that although Joe Paterno has accumulated more Division I-A wins than any coach in major college football history (keeping in mind that 31 of Bobby Bowden's victories were as coach of Samford, a Division I-AA team), he has had his ups and downs over the years. What some may not realize is that these ups and downs have come in predictable cycles, with each cycle in the sixties, seventies, and eighties lasting four to five years and each cycle thereafter lasting two to three years. Although each cycle has its unique characteristics, there is a general pattern composed of three phases of progress. These phases are described next, followed by summaries of each of the 11 "cycles of excellence" comprising the history of Penn State football during the Paterno era.

Phase I: "Out of Whack"

Each cycle begins with a year or two in which various obstacles to excellence become apparent early in the season. In some cases the obstacles reflect recruiting gaps, injuries, or other personnel problems. In other cases the obstacles are more psychological in nature and point to problems with focus, confidence, or a lack of team chemistry. Often these obstacles are magnified by a tough schedule and some bad luck.

Phase II: "Lions' Pride"

In the second phase of each cycle, the team makes significant progress in addressing the obstacles that caused it to get "out of whack" for a while. New recruits join the team, inexperienced players become experienced players, the coaching staff tightens its preparation routines, senior leaders emerge, and although the Lions still lose an occasional game,

Paterno encourages his team during the first half of the 2003 Ohio State game at State College. *Photo courtesy of AP/Wide World Photos.*

there is a feeling that the team is on track and will soon compete for a national title.

Phase III: "King of Beasts"

In the last phase of the cycle, the team has exceptional talent at several key positions and a solid supporting cast, strong leadership from both the players and coaching staff, and a sense of destiny. The team has a robust sense of confidence derived from its ability to make big plays and successfully overcome adversity. These are the years that produce the highest rankings, the greatest heroes, and the most cherished memories. At least 13 of Joe Paterno's 38 teams can be regarded as having earned "King of Beasts" status, as evidenced by either an 11-win season, a top 5 ranking, or being in serious contention for a national title for most of the season.

Paterno's Formula for Excellence

Careful analysis of the Nittany Lion teams that have achieved "King of Beasts" status reveals two common themes that together constitute the Joe Paterno "formula for excellence." These are the essential ingredients for achieving the highest levels of success in the Penn State system designed by coach Paterno.

1. **Two outstanding running backs capable of gaining at least 1,400 yards in career rushing, with at least one at the 2,000-plus career level.** Penn State must have at least one running back who can be counted on to chew up yardage, sustain drives, and score touchdowns, and another who can offer similar productivity, even if only in a backup or supporting role, to ensure that the offense does not become too one-dimensional. This ingredient for success of course also implies the presence of a competent offensive line capable of providing great backs with some room to run.

2. **Several dominating linebackers and defensive linemen capable of earning All-American status at some point in their careers.** The Paterno philosophy requires the up-front defenders to control their opponents through intimidating defensive pressure, consistent tackling, and game-changing plays. Ideally, these outstanding defensive players are distributed throughout the defensive line and linebacker positions rather than being clustered along just one line of defense.

11 Cycles of Excellence

Penn State football is currently approaching the middle of its 11th cycle of excellence during the Paterno era. Cycle one started with a bang, as Penn State reeled off 30 games without a loss from early 1967 through the end of 1969. The case for No. 1 was particularly strong in 1969, but the chance for a fair vote was undermined by President Nixon's locker-room declaration of Texas as the national champion after the Longhorns completed their undefeated season against Arkansas.

Cycle two ended in 1973 with a Heisman Trophy for star running back John Cappelletti, which helped ease the frustration of being ranked only No. 5 (due to a relatively easy schedule) despite a perfect 12–0 season.

Cycle three (1974–1978) was unusual in that the Out of Whack phase turned into a three-year slide, but the program got back on track by enjoying two consecutive King of Beasts years. However, the cycle ended in disappointing fashion as Penn State—ranked No. 1 in the major polls for the first time in its history—came up just short in a Sugar Bowl showdown with No. 2 Alabama. Fortunately, that disappointment was short-lived as Penn State quickly regrouped in cycle four (1979–1982) to win its first consensus national title (in 1982) in a tense Sugar Bowl matchup against top-ranked Georgia.

Cycle five (1983–1986) was perhaps even more glorious, as Paterno won his second national championship (in 1986) in one of the most famous games in college football history, the Fiesta Bowl "Duel in the Desert" against a flashy but fragile Miami team.

Like the third cycle, cycle six (1987–1991) took five years to complete and ended with some regret about "what might have been" had the Lions been able to make a key play or two in a particularly crucial game—a midseason loss to eventual co-national champion Miami. Things changed, however, when the Lions became a member of the Big Ten conference. The Paterno "cycles of excellence" began operating in a compressed two-to-three-year time frame, consistent with the more rapid evolutionary pace that has characterized major college football teams during the past decade.

In the first cycle of this new era (cycle seven, 1992–1994), the Lions were able to recapture the glory of their finest years with one of the most potent offensive attacks in the history of college football, culminating in a perfect 12–0 record and a No. 1 ranking in virtually every objective (mathematically based) rating system.

Penn State had so many great returning players in 1995 that the team was able to bypass the Out of Whack phase in cycle eight (1995–1996) and rack up another 11-win season in 1996. The next year looked even brighter as Penn State was ranked No. 1 for a while, but a season-ending injury to running back Aaron Harris disrupted the team's offensive schemes, essentially forcing Paterno to go back one step and again start a new cycle.

Cycle nine (1997–1999) continued with a solid year in 1998 and a very serious run at a national title in 1999, when the Lions were ranked No. 2 throughout most of the season. However, a stunning late-season miracle by Minnesota triggered a bewildering three-game losing streak that kept one of Penn State's finest teams from being able to fully realize its King of Beasts status.

Heavy graduation losses led to a pair of Out of Whack seasons (in 2000–2001) to start cycle 10, but by 2002 it was clear that Penn State was again ready to rejoin the college football elite. Unfortunately, a series of agonizingly close defeats, including two overtime losses, kept this team in the Lions' Pride phase, and for the first time a cycle was completed without a culminating King of Beasts year.

Cycle 11 started (in 2003) with the first nine-loss season in Penn State history, but this performance is not so unusual when seen in the context of Paterno's cycles of excellence. A down year was predictable given a tough schedule, the loss of four NFL first-round draft choices, and the fact that the 1999 recruiting class included barely 10 players, with only a handful making significant contributions in 2003. Nevertheless, given the outstanding young talent the team is developing and the favorable upcoming schedules, one can realistically expect an escalation to Lions' Pride

Lydell Mitchell, shown in 1970, was one of the first in a long line of great running backs to play for Paterno. *Photo courtesy of AP/Wide World Photos.*

JOE PATERNO'S 11 CYCLES OF EXCELLENCE

	Out of Whack	Lions' Pride	King of Beasts
Cycle 1	1966 (5–5, NR)	1967 (8–2–1, No. 10)	1968 (11–0, No. 2)
			1969 (11–0, No. 2)
Cycle 2	1970 (7–3, No. 18)	1971 (11–1, No. 5)[a]	
		1972 (10–2, No. 10)	1973 (12–0, No. 5)
Cycle 3	1974 (10–2, No. 7)[b]		
	1975 (9–3, No. 10)[b]		
	1976 (7–5, NR)	[*skipped phase*]	1977 (11–1, No. 5)
			1978 (11–1, No. 4)
Cycle 4	1979 (8–4, No. 20)	1980 (10–2, No. 8)	1981 (10–2, No. 3)
			1982 (11–1, No. 1)
Cycle 5	1983 (8–4–1, NR)		
	1984 (6–5, NR)	[*skipped phase*]	1985 (11–1, No. 3)
			1986 (12–0, No. 1)
Cycle 6	1987 (8–4, NR)		
	1988 (5–6, NR)	1989 (8–3–1, No. 15)	
		1990 (9–3, No. 11)	1991 (11–2, No. 3)
Cycle 7	1992 (7–5, No. 24)	1993 (10–2, No. 8)	1994 (12–0, No. 2)
Cycle 8	[*skipped phase*]	1995 (9–3, No. 13)	1996 (11–2, No. 7)
Cycle 9	[*skipped phase*]	1997 (9–3, No. 16)	
		1998 (9–3, No. 17)	1999 (9–0 start, No. 2)[c]
			1999 (10–3, No. 11)[c]
Cycle 10	2000 (5–7, NR)		
	2001 (5–6, NR)	2002 (9–4, No. 15)	[*skipped phase*]
Cycle 11	2003 (3–9, NR)	2004 (TBD)	2005 (TBD)

[a] In 1971 Penn State played only one highly ranked team during the regular season (Tennessee) and lost 31–11, suggesting that they were not yet at the King of Beasts level.

[b] Although the wins were frequent in 1974 and 1975, most were earned against relatively weak teams during a downward trajectory, thus suggesting an extended Out of Whack phase.

[c] In 1999 Penn State started 9–0, was ranked No. 2 for most of the year, and played seven ranked teams, beating four. Three late-season defeats were initiated by a fluke play and were all very close losses.

status in 2004 (i.e., at least eight to nine wins in a 12-game season) followed by a national title run in 2005. The key question is whether coach Paterno will have the right mix of players to implement his formula for excellence and to cultivate the kind of commitment and leadership needed to field a championship team. We believe the answer to this question is yes. That is why we boldly predict that history is about to repeat itself. In 2005 Penn State will win at least 11 games, be ranked in the top 5, and be in serious contention for No. 1.

Cycle One (1966–1969): The Jayhawk Jaywalk

Out of Whack. When Joe Paterno was named head coach in 1966, he inherited one of the most difficult schedules in Penn State history. He had to play the No. 1 team in the country, Michigan State, in just the second game of his coaching career (losing 42–8). Crushing defeats by No. 4 UCLA (49–11) and No. 5 Georgia Tech (21–0) followed in this difficult year of on-the-job training.

Lions' Pride. A tough one-point loss to Navy in the first game of the 1967 season led Paterno to engage in some soul-searching and radical thinking. In the off-season he had developed a revolutionary 4-4-3 defense, but he wondered if he had the athletes in place to execute it. In a game widely cited as the beginning of the Paterno legend, he played a group of talented sopho-

mores who would go on to become the nucleus of his great undefeated teams of 1968 and 1969. In that game, the new-look Lions stuffed highly regarded Miami 17–8, then scared Heisman Trophy–winning quarterback Gary Beban and his No. 2 UCLA Bruins in a 17–15 loss. They subsequently shut down No. 3 North Carolina State in a defensive struggle (13–8) defined by a heroic last-minute goal-line defensive stop at the 1-yard line that many regard as one of the top 10 plays in Penn State football history.

Penn State's seven-game winning streak was interrupted by a Gator Bowl tie with Florida State in which an overly bold young coach lost a 17–0 lead after a failed fourth-and-1 play in Penn State territory (at the 15-yard line!) led to two momentum-changing scores. Nevertheless, the Lions maintained an unbeaten streak that would stretch to a phenomenal 31 games before the next Out of Whack phase began in 1970.

King of Beasts. The 1968 team combined an awesome defensive group led by three future Hall of Famers—linebackers Dennis Onkotz and Jack Ham and defensive lineman Mike Reid—with a multifaceted offense led by high school teammates Ted Kwalick (a future Hall of Fame tight end) and quarterback Chuck Burkhart. With the majority of opponents unable to score in double digits, the Lions methodically racked up 10 straight wins and earned a bid to the Orange Bowl, where they beat Kansas 15–14 in one of the most dramatic finishes in college football history. Many fans still recall the pure joy they felt when Penn State scored a last-minute touchdown and game-winning two-point conversion after the Jayhawks were flagged for having 12 men on the field on the Lions' initial conversion attempt.

In 1969 all of Paterno's superstar defenders returned, and the Lions once again mowed down 11 consecutive opponents. Penn State allowed three or fewer points in five games, including a 10–3 Orange Bowl win over Missouri, and was named co-national champion by the Massey Ratings and the Foundation for the Analysis of Competitions and Tournaments.

Paterno's formula for excellence: two outstanding running backs and several dominating linebackers and defensive linemen. In 1968 Charlie Pittman (2,236 career yards, 30 touchdowns) was the leading rusher, with Bob Campbell (1,480 career yards, 14 touchdowns) in a strong supporting role. In 1969 two super sophomores—Lydell Mitchell (2,934 career yards, 38 touchdowns) and Franco Harris (2,002 career yards, 24 touchdowns)—joined Pittman to form one of the most talented backfields ever seen in college football. On defense, in addition to the awesome threesome of Onkotz, Ham, and Reid, defensive tackle Steve Smear and safety Neal Smith earned All-American status in 1969 on a team that could not have been more deserving of a national championship.

Cycle Two (1970–1973): Something for Joe, Something for Joey

Out of Whack. The Nittany Lions won their first outing in 1970 to stretch their amazing unbeaten streak to 31 games. However, they then lost three of their next four contests as the defense struggled to adjust to heavy graduation losses and the offense sputtered in the wake of a quarterback controversy. Coach Paterno boldly inserted third-string sophomore quarterback John Hufnagel into a midseason starting role, and the future All-American responded by leading Penn State to five easy victories to salvage a 7–3 season.

Lions' Pride. The Lions enjoyed two very good seasons in 1971 and 1972, especially 1971 when Lydell Mitchell set three NCAA scoring records and the team had some of the most productive offensive numbers in Penn State history. However, Tennessee thwarted their aspirations for greatness by ruining an otherwise perfect regular season both years. The Tennessee games were critical because few other challenging teams were on the schedule to provide a true measure of greatness. The 1971 team made a strong case for King of Beasts status when they blew out No. 12 Texas 30–6 in the Cotton Bowl, but even that outstanding victory could not fully erase the disappointment of the 31–11 loss to Tennessee in the regular-season finale. The 1972 team played second-ranked Oklahoma in the Sugar Bowl but lost 14–0 in a game whose score might easily have been

John Cappelletti, with help from Paterno and entertainer Bob Hope, admires the Heisman Trophy awarded to him in 1973. *Photo courtesy of AP/Wide World Photos.*

reversed had star running back John Cappelletti not been forced to sit out the game with a viral infection.

King of Beasts. After the 1972 season, Joe Paterno almost didn't make it to the pinnacle of his second cycle of excellence that was to follow in 1973. The New England Patriots made a lucrative offer that was so tempting that Paterno actually accepted it before changing his mind the following morning. Perhaps he dreamed about the bumper stickers, postcards, and special buttons distributed all over town by the "Mother Button Maker" (also known as Mimi Fredman), who had just that season initiated what has since become one of the longest-running marketing campaigns in the history of advertising with the invention of the bank-sponsored Penn State football buttons. Her simple but compelling slogan "Don't Go, Joe" was a heartfelt wish from the entire community that Paterno could not ignore. In his press conference announcing his unexpected change of heart, Paterno's message was essentially the same as that printed on the very first bowl game button that year: "I'd Sooner Be a Nittany Lion."

The 1973 regular season provided great enjoyment for Nittany Lion fans but relatively little drama, as Penn State dominated virtually every opponent on the way to another perfect season. The postseason was another story, as the Lions won their third Orange Bowl in six years in a tense matchup with LSU, and John Cappelletti was awarded the Heisman Trophy and Maxwell Award. At the Heisman presentation, Cappelletti's tearful tribute to his 11-year-old brother, Joey, who was in the audience that night despite suffering from leukemia, was so moving that it became the basis for a television movie called *Something for Joey*. Joey died in April 1976, but the memory of his brother's dedication will be embedded in the collective memory of Penn State fans forever.

Paterno's formula for excellence: two outstanding running backs and several dominating linebackers and defensive linemen. Cappelletti (2,639 career yards, 29 touchdowns) led the 1973 team to a 12–0 record while running behind three All-American offensive linemen: tackle Charlie Getty, guard Mark Markovich, and tight end Dan Natale. Tom Donchez (1,422 career yards, 11 touchdowns) provided effective backup help. In addition, the 1973 squad had multiple All-American caliber players at linebacker and on the defensive line. The biggest stars were linebacker Ed O'Neil and defensive tackles Randy Crowder and Mike Hartenstine, but linebacker Greg Buttle and defensive end Greg Murphy also contributed to one of the strongest defensive fronts in PSU history.

Cycle Three (1974–1978): The Simple Bear Necessities

Out of Whack. With 10 NFL draftees among those departing after 1973's season of perfection, and with no star running back to plug into Paterno's formula for excellence, it was perhaps inevitable that a longer-than-usual rebuilding process would be needed before the Lions were fully equipped to contend for a national title. Indeed, Penn State's record actually became worse for three consecutive years—the only time that has ever happened in the Paterno era. In 1974 an inexperienced team was only six points from an undefeated season, but they struggled in losses to Navy (in heavy rain) and North Carolina State. The 1975 squad was also inconsistent, as they won nine games but were defeated by two top 5 teams (Ohio State and Alabama) and were upset again by North Carolina State as the result of a rare missed field goal by superstar kicker Chris Bahr. The Lions bottomed out in 1976 with five losses against a difficult schedule that included the No. 1 and No. 2 ranked teams in the country (Ohio State and Pitt).

Lions' Pride. By 1977 coach Paterno had once again assembled the raw materials needed for a run at a national championship, and the team jumped over this phase of the cycle.

King of Beasts. Both the 1977 and 1978 Penn State teams finished the season with a top 5 ranking and an 11–1 record, and the stars for each team were essentially the same, including All-Americans on defense (linemen Bruce Clark and Matt Millen and safety Pete Harris), offense (quarterback Chuck Fusina and tackle Keith Dorney),

and special teams (kicker Matt Bahr). However, the course of each season could not have been any different. In 1977 the Lions lost their fourth game (to Kentucky, 24–20) and struggled for a while until catching fire at the end of the season to finish on a high note. In contrast, the only time the 1978 team seemed to be in danger of losing was in its opening game to Temple (10–7), thanks to an awesome defense that pitched three shutouts and held eight opponents to 10 points or less. But in a battle of No. 1 versus No. 2 in the Sugar Bowl, Alabama's defense had the last word, as late in the game they stopped two rushing attempts from inside the 1-yard line that might have produced the game-tying score. Paterno's best team yet had failed to hold onto its top ranking as a result of a sequence of plays that has produced more second-guessing than any other coaching decision in Penn State history.

Paterno's formula for excellence: two outstanding running backs and several dominating linebackers and defensive linemen. Matt Suhey (2,818 career yards, 26 touchdowns), Booker Moore (2,072 career yards, 20 touchdowns), and four other running backs with more than 1,000 career rushing yards were the primary ground gainers during this phase of the cycle. Their success was attributable in large part to an offensive line filled with All-Americans (tackle Keith Dorney, guard Randy Sidler, and tight end Mickey Shuler). The PSU defense was led by Bruce Clark

Paterno is carried off the field following the Nittany Lions' 27–23 defeat of Georgia in the Sugar Bowl to claim the 1982 national championship. *Photo courtesy of AP/Wide World Photos.*

and Matt Millen, one of the greatest tackle combinations in college football history, with All-American linebacker Lance Mehl providing additional muscle behind the defensive line.

Cycle Four (1979-1982): How Sweet It Is!

Out of Whack. Most of the stars in Paterno's 1978 formula for excellence returned the following year, which may lead one to wonder why the 8-4 1979 team was not more successful. Although All-American quarterback Chuck Fusina was hard to replace, the biggest problem may have been an inexperienced offensive line, as the defense continued to hold most opponents to single digits. With the offense Out of Whack most of the season, the Lion defense was not able to dominate the better teams on the schedule as they had done in previous years.

Lions' Pride. The 1980 squad began the season with high hopes but not high expectations given the number of underclassmen in key positions. Todd Blackledge eventually won the battle of inexperienced quarterbacks over Jeff Hostetler, and future offensive superstars Curt Warner (running back) and Kenny Jackson (wide receiver) began to reveal their game-breaking potential. However, the young offense was quite erratic, scoring more than 29 points in only two regular-season games, and had to depend heavily on a tough, experienced defense to cover for their mistakes. Nevertheless, the team suffered defeat only twice—in each case to a top 5 team—and they showed great resilience in a big Fiesta Bowl victory over Ohio State, where they rebounded from a 19-10 halftime deficit to pull out a memorable 31-19 win.

King of Beasts. The 1981 and 1982 Nittany Lions were capable of beating the best teams in the country—and frequently did so. However, the schedule had become so difficult that it was unrealistic to expect a perfect season even with the powerhouse offense Paterno had put together. The tough schedule played to the Lions' advantage, however. They were ranked No. 3 in 1981 (and No. 1 in the Dunkel System and Sagarin Ratings) despite two losses, and were given an opportunity to play for the national title in 1982 against No. 1 Georgia despite a midseason loss to Alabama. Indeed, the 1982 team was the first in NCAA history to end the season as the top-ranked team while playing the most difficult schedule in the NCAA.

The Sugar Bowl victory over Georgia that brought Paterno his first consensus national title is, of course, widely cited as one of the greatest games in Penn State history. However, many would argue that two regular-season games in this cycle were equally special. In the final regular-season game in 1981, the underrated (No. 11) Lions ventured into Pitt Stadium to take on the nation's top-ranked team, led by All-American quarterback Dan Marino. With the Panthers leading 14-0 and driving for another score, Penn State began forcing turnovers and making big plays on offense in an amazing sequence that included one of the most entertaining plays any Penn State fan could hope to witness, a sideline tiptoe catch and pirouette by Kenny Jackson for the go-ahead touchdown. All-American safety Mark Robinson's 91-yard interception return wrapped up the huge 48–14 victory that made it clear who was the true King of Beasts in the East.

Two even more memorable plays occurred just five games later, as the Nittany Lions hosted the No. 2 ranked Nebraska Cornhuskers in a make-or-break game for Penn State's title aspirations. Trailing 24–21 with 13 seconds left to play and 17 yards from the end zone, quarterback Todd Blackledge threw a highly controversial 15-yard completion to tight end Mike McCloskey that may have been caught out of bounds. One play later, backup tight end Kirk "Stonehands" Bowman famously scooped up a disputed low touchdown pass to complete "The Miracle of Mount Nittany."

Paterno's formula for excellence: two outstanding running backs and several dominating linebackers and defensive linemen. The powerful 1981 team and the 1982 national champions were led by Penn State's all-time career rushing leader, Curt Warner (3,398 yards, 24 touchdowns), with strong support from Jon Williams (2,042 career yards, 14 touchdowns). Their efforts made it possible for a big-play passing attack led by quarterback Todd Blackledge and wide receiver Kenny Jackson to thrive. In an unexpected twist for a Paterno-coached team, the running game provided such a reliable foundation for the rest of the offense that Penn State ended up becoming the first team in NCAA history to win a national title while accumulating more passing than rushing yardage over the course of the season. Although the 1982 defense gave up more points than most of Penn State's superstar teams, the essential ingredients for playing championship football against top-flight competition were in place both at linebacker, where Harry Hamilton and Scott Radecic offered inspired leadership, and on the defensive line, where Walker Lee Ashley earned All-American status at defensive end.

Cycle Five (1983–1986): Bent, But Never Broken

Out of Whack. With Curt Warner, Todd Blackledge, and a number of other star players lost to graduation, the Lions lost their first three games in 1983 before clawing back to a semirespectable 8-4-1 record that featured an inspiring 34–28 victory over No. 3 Alabama. That game ended with a decisive fourth-down stop on the 1-yard line that allowed the Lions to get some measure of revenge for the 1979 Sugar Bowl loss.

Things continued to look promising the next fall when Penn State opened with three wins. But that was a mirage as the 1984 Lions failed to score more than 14 points in five of their last eight games and barely finished the season with a winning record (6-5).

Lions' Pride. The slow rebuilding process accelerated in 1985 beyond all expectations, and as a result Paterno was again able to bypass the Lions' Pride phase in cycle five.

King of Beasts. The 1985 season was possibly the most surprising year in Paterno's storied history, as he coached a team full of underclassmen to a perfect regular season in which they won three of their first six games by just two points and none by more than a touchdown. After beating up on Notre Dame and Pitt to finish the season, the No. 1 Lions had another shot at a national title against No. 2 Oklahoma in the Orange Bowl. Penn State lost 25–10, but with almost all of the team's best players returning in 1986, disappointment almost immediately turned into anticipation.

Andre Collins (left) and Blair Thomas celebrate Penn State's 1986 national championship at a State College rally that drew an estimated 30,000 well-wishers. *Photo courtesy of AP/Wide World Photos.*

And with good reason! In the Nittany Lions' 100th year of football, they celebrated a "Century of Excellence" by subduing every challenger, including not only No. 2 Alabama in an eye-opening midseason pounding, but also No. 1 Miami in a monumental Fiesta Bowl triumph that gave Paterno his second consensus national title. In that game, a conservative Penn State offense was able to generate only 162 yards and eight first downs while the "bad boys" from Miami racked up 445 yards and 22 first downs. However, with a stunning (pun intended) secondary led by safety Ray Isom and cornerback Duffy Cobbs backing up some of the toughest linemen and smartest linebackers ever to wear a blue-and-white uniform, the Hurricanes could not convert their blustery attack into points. With Penn State nursing a precarious 14–10 lead going into the final moments of battle, the game came down to a spine-tingling goal-line stand that ended with linebacker Pete Giftopoulos cradling the game-winning interception (quarterback Vinny Testaverde's fifth completion to the wrong team), thus preserving the victory for the Lions in one of the greatest college football games ever played.

Paterno's formula for excellence: two outstanding running backs and several dominating linebackers and defensive linemen. At least in terms of career rushing yardage, the 1986 team had the greatest one-two punch of all, with senior D. J. Dozier (3,227 yards, 25 touchdowns) leading the charge and sophomore Blair Thomas (3,301 yards, 21 touchdowns) playing a supporting role. In addition, coach Paterno could turn to two of the best fullbacks in Penn State history, Steve Smith (1,246 career yards, 11 touchdowns) and Tim Manoa (1,098 yards, 5 touchdowns), and a solid offensive line led by tackle Chris Conlin and guard Steve Wisniewski to come up with tough yardage in the clutch. On the defensive front, amazingly, every Penn State opponent scored fewer than 20 points. Among the many defensive heroes on this outstanding team, four All-Americans stood out as the best of the best: linebackers Shane Conlan and Trey Bauer and defensive tackles Tim Johnson and Pete Curkendall. The combined talent and reliability of a truly great defense and a solid running game gave coach Paterno a team perfectly suited to his preferred style of play.

Cycle Six (1987–1991): Flawed, but Brilliant

Out of Whack. The first two years of cycle six were almost identical to the previous cycle. Despite heavy losses to graduation, the 1987 team accumulated a passable 8–4 record, including an exciting win against seventh-ranked Notre Dame that compensated for several disappointing losses to ranked teams. However, things got worse in 1988 as the Lions played a brutal schedule and were only able to outscore 5 of their 11 opponents. Amazingly, this was Penn State's first losing season in 50 years.

Lions' Pride. After the 1989 squad lost its opener to Virginia for its sixth loss in seven games, concerns about Paterno's leadership abilities escalated. However, the veteran coach quickly responded with a five-game winning streak that ended only because sixth-ranked Alabama was able to block a last-second, chip-shot field goal to escape with a 17–16 victory. A subsequent loss to No. 1 Notre Dame was offset by a wild and wacky Holiday Bowl victory against BYU (50–39) that boosted PSU to a solid No. 15 ranking.

The 1990 season yielded more upward movement in the polls, as the Lions shook off an 0–2 start to win the last nine games on their regular-season schedule, including a stunning 24–21 win over No. 1 Notre Dame in which Penn State fought back from a 21–7 halftime deficit while never allowing the Fighting Irish to cross midfield in the second half. That led to a Blockbuster Bowl showdown with Bobby Bowden's sixth-ranked Florida State Seminoles. Unfortunately, the Lions lost an opportunity to make an argument for a No. 1 ranking of their own when a mistake-filled 24–17 defeat dropped them to No. 11 in the final AP poll.

King of Beasts. The mood in Happy Valley was upbeat the following autumn as Penn State, led by experienced quarterback Tony Sacca, dominated the defending national champion (Georgia Tech) in their season opener (34–22). The Lions then clobbered most of the other teams on their schedule, including highly ranked Notre Dame (35–13). However, the pass-oriented offense was not designed using Paterno's preferred formula for excellence, and as a result the team lacked the consistency needed to take the final step to a national title. This was revealed in an early loss to USC and a critical game with No. 2 Miami that would have positioned the Lions for a bigger postseason prize if they could have scored just one more time in the fourth quarter. Nevertheless, pollsters were so impressed with Penn State's explosive 41–17 victory over Tennessee in the Fiesta Bowl that they ranked the Lions No. 3 in the final polls despite their two earlier defeats.

Paterno's formula for excellence: two outstanding running backs and several dominating linebackers and defensive linemen. The 1991 team had an explosive passing attack but fewer weapons at running back than most of Paterno's best teams, with Richie Anderson (1,756 yards, 29 touchdowns) the leading ground gainer. The vulnerability was small but perhaps enough to cost the Lions a national title. On defense, Penn State had impact players throughout its lineup. However, other than defensive tackle Lou Benfatti, none of the very talented linemen or linebackers earned All-American status, as the team's most consistent players were safety Darren Perry and wide receiver O. J. McDuffie.

Running back Ki-Jana Carter leaves the field after the Nittany Lions' come-from-behind 35–31 victory at Illinois, which secured the Big Ten championship in the team's second year in the conference. *Photo courtesy of AP/Wide World Photos.*

Cycle Seven (1992–1994): The Irresistible Force

Out of Whack. The 1992 season was fascinating because Penn State was locked out of not only the bowls associated with the Big Ten (since the Lions would not begin conference play until the following year), but also the bowls affiliated with the new Bowl Coalition (since the Big Ten was not a part of that pre-BCS agreement). In a bold move designed to ensure that they wouldn't be sitting at home over the holidays, Penn State accepted an invitation to play in the Blockbuster Bowl—three months before the start of the season! That meant that the team would not be playing for a conference title, a bowl game, or any of the other usual incentives that define a season. The only goal they had to play for was a national title, which effectively meant they had to win all 11 games since they were unlikely to be paired against a top-ranked team in the Blockbuster Bowl.

The season progressed in promising fashion for the first five games, as the Lions scored an average of 42 points while rising to a No. 5 ranking. At that point they were poised to become a serious factor in the national title race with a win over No. 2 Miami, and Penn State did in fact appear to be the better team that day, outgaining Miami 370 to 218 yards and dominating time of possession. However, injured place-kicker Craig Fayak missed several field goals, and quarterback John Sacca threw an interception that was returned for a touchdown on the game's decisive play, and the Lions lost both the game (17–14) and their sense of purpose. The team went on to lose four of their remaining six games, including a lackluster defeat to Stanford in the Blockbuster Bowl.

Lions' Pride. Penn State celebrated its entry into the Big Ten with a solid outing against Minnesota (38–20), then followed that up with four very impressive wins. The Lions' progress was disrupted by the stunning midseason departure of quarterback John Sacca (after being benched in favor of future superstar quarterback Kerry Collins) and by consecutive losses to the "Big Two" of the Big Ten, Michigan and Ohio State. However, Paterno and his team leaders vowed that they would not follow the 1992 script. They rebounded with five inspired victories, including a 38–37 miracle comeback against Michigan State (after falling behind 37–17 late in the third quarter) and a 31–13 drubbing of Tennessee in the Citrus Bowl that previewed what was about to happen in the next glorious season.

King of Beasts. You had to see it to believe it. The 1994 offense was so potent and had so many weapons that you could not leave your seat for even a minute when they had the ball. One of the most productive offense in NCAA history racked up an average of 47 points per game (more than 55 in five games) and featured four First Team All-Americans—running back Ki-Jana Carter, quarterback Kerry Collins, wide receiver Bobby Engram,

and tight end Kyle Brady. Penn State rose to No. 1 after holding off No. 5 Michigan 31–24 and crushing No. 14 Ohio State 63–14. However, they dropped to No. 2 for the remainder of the year after a blowout win over Indiana turned into a close-looking contest on the scoreboard (35–29) when the Hoosiers scored a couple of last-minute touchdowns against the Lion reserves. Even an incredible

Penn State's LaVar Arrington, now an NFL superstar with the Washington Redskins, moves in to drop Arizona's Dennis Northcutt during a game in 1999. *Photo courtesy of AP/Wide World Photos.*

35–31 comeback win against Illinois that featured "The Drive," a 96-yard, late fourth-quarter thing of beauty that saved the Lions' perfect season, could not persuade the pollsters to vote the best team No. 1. Nevertheless, after beating Oregon 38–20 in the Rose Bowl, Penn State was declared national champion by at least eight different organizations using objective rating systems—*The New York Times*, the Sagarin Ratings, the National Championship Foundation, the Matthews Grid Ratings, the Foundation for the Analysis of Competitions and Tournaments, the DeVold System, the Massey Ratings, and the Billingsley Report.

Paterno's formula for excellence: two outstanding running backs and several dominating linebackers and defensive linemen. In 1994 the featured back was Ki-Jana Carter (2,829 career yards, 34 touchdowns), with Mike Archie (1,694 career yards, 14 touchdowns) and Stephen Pitts (1,156 career yards, 5 touchdowns) contributing significant yardage along with fullbacks Brian Milne (512 career yards, 16 touchdowns) and Jon Witman (366 career yards, 15 touchdowns), who frequently finished off scoring drives. The Lions also had two All-American anchors on the offensive line: tight end Kyle Brady and guard Jeff Hartings.

The 1994 team's No. 2 ranking was an irrational result that reflected the voters' desire to give the national title to the sentimental favorite, Nebraska coach Tom Osborne, rather than to the team that had the most impressive wins against the most difficult schedule. When asked to explain their dubious vote, many pollsters cited the fact that Penn State's opponents routinely scored between 21 and 31 points, but they didn't take into account that many of those points were scored against third- and fourth-string players after the Lions' quick-strike offense had racked up a big lead. Consistent with this unappreciative view, none of the PSU defenders on this great team earned All-American status in 1994 or in subsequent years, with the exception of safety Kim Herring.

Cycle Eight (1995–1996): Overcoming Adversity

Out of Whack. Although a number of star players completed their college careers in 1994, enough firepower remained on the 1995 squad to enable the Nittany Lions to bypass the Out of Whack phase in cycle eight.

Lions' Pride. Penn State ran its winning streak to 20 games with a 3–0 start, but then reality set in as the Lions fell to three of their first six Big Ten opponents, including No. 5 Ohio State and No. 6 Northwestern. Penn State responded in resilient fashion to finish the season with an impressive three-game winning streak that started with the Lions overcoming Michigan (and a 17-inch snowfall) and ended with an Outback Bowl pounding of No. 12 Auburn.

King of Beasts. The 1996 edition of the Nittany Lions had the look and feel of a Joe Paterno championship team, with most of the starting defense returning and a strong running back anchoring the offense. Consistent with these high expectations, Penn State began the season with an easy win over a top 10 team (No. 7 USC) and continued into October with a 5–0 record. However, a bad day against No. 3 Ohio State and a 21–20 upset loss to Iowa dampened the team's aspirations, and Penn State was again forced to respond to midseason adversity. The Lions showed both their character

Larry Johnson breaks free for a touchdown against Louisiana Tech early in the 2002 season. *Photo courtesy of AP/Wide World Photos.*

and their talent by winning all five of their remaining games, including big wins over three ranked teams: Northwestern, Michigan, and Texas, with the latter game enabling coach Paterno to run his amazing Fiesta Bowl record to 6–0.

Paterno's formula for excellence: two outstanding running backs and several dominating linebackers and defensive linemen. Penn State had one of its most productive running backs, Curtis Enis (3,256 career yards, 36 touchdowns), leading the way in 1996. A young Aaron Harris (1,166 career yards, 19 touchdowns) provided the Lions with yet another powerful weapon, as he led the team in rushing average with 5.6 yards per carry. On defense, linebacker Brandon Short and defensive end Courtney Brown added significant depth to a team with solid experience but only one defensive superstar, safety Kim Herring.

Cycle Nine (1997–1999): Golden Opportunity

Out of Whack. Although the 1997 Lions were definitely Out of Whack at the end of the season, they played so well for most of the year that they clearly merit Lions' Pride status.

Lions' Pride. In 1997 Penn State started the season in the No. 1 position. The Lions definitely looked the part when they knocked off No. 7 Ohio State in game five, 31–27, behind the powerful running of Curtis Enis and Aaron Harris. However, Harris suffered a season-ending ACL injury early in the next game, and after that the offense was never the same, as the Lions averaged only 22 points per outing after scoring 44 per game during the first half of the year. The once promising season ended at 9–3 with a blowout loss to Michigan State (49–14) and a Citrus Bowl loss to Florida (21–6). Star wide receiver Joe Jurevicius had to sit out the bowl game for academic reasons, and Enis missed it due to an NCAA violation (accepting clothing gifts from a sports agent).

The 1998 team also finished 9–3, although in a more predictable fashion. Penn State easily beat most of the teams on its schedule but lacked the firepower needed to handle the Big Ten's elite defensive teams (Ohio State, Michigan, and Wisconsin), which collectively allowed the Lions to score only 12 points against them.

King of Beasts. Penn State entered the 1999 season with high expectations. The Lions had some of the best defensive players in the country coming back for their final season while also fielding a balanced, multidimensional offense. In game four, a huge win at Miami (27–23) that was saved by a long touchdown pass from quarterback Kevin Thompson to wide receiver Chafie Fields in the waning moments of the game, suggested that this might be another Paterno team of destiny. The wins piled up, and soon Penn State was about to improve its record to 10–0 as the defense forced a tenacious Minnesota team into a desperation fourth-and-18 pass from beyond field-goal range.

But oh, no! The ball was deflected and Gopher wide receiver Arland Bruce made a miraculous shoestring catch, setting up the winning field goal (24–23) and dashing PSU's championship aspirations. The stunned Lions suffered two more close losses before recovering with a 24–0 Alamo Bowl victory over Texas A&M, which seemed like a truer representation of this star-studded team.

Paterno's formula for excellence: two outstanding running backs and several dominating linebackers and defensive linemen. The featured back in 1999 was sophomore Eric McCoo (2,518 career yards, 18 touchdowns), with freshman Larry Johnson (2,953 career yards, 26 touchdowns) being one of several players providing backup help. However, in terms of individual talent, no Penn State team had brighter stars than the defensive leaders on the 1999 squad. In addition to All-American linebacker Brandon Short, the Lions had the No. 1 and No. 2 selections in the 2000 NFL Draft in defensive end Courtney Brown and linebacker Lavar Arrington. Arrington also won the Butkus Award as the nation's premier linebacker and the Chuck Bednarik Award as the nation's top defensive player.

Cycle 10 (2000–2002): The Best of Times, the Worst of Overtimes

Out of Whack. If ever a season was out of whack, 2000 was the year. The season started with quarterback Rashard Casey under suspicion for

assaulting a police officer, an allegation that both coach Paterno and later a grand jury flatly rejected. This distraction no doubt contributed to the Lions' inability to score more than six points in four of their first five games. Then, freshman cornerback Adam Taliaferro suffered a devastating cervical spine injury that ended his football career. Penn State rebounded to win four of its last seven games, but it was not enough to avoid Paterno's second losing season in 35 years.

Better things were expected in 2001, and the year did indeed start off on a joyous note as Adam Taliaferro was able to lead his teammates out of the Beaver Stadium tunnel to open the season. However, the Lion offense could not seem to get organized behind quarterback Matt Senneca, and Paterno finally had to insert freshman quarterback Zack Mills to try to improve the team's scoring potential. The move worked, as the offense went from an average of 8 points per game to more than 30. In fact, Penn State was remarkably close to running the table after its 0–4 start. The team won five of its last seven games—including a thrilling 29–27 comeback defeat of Ohio State that enabled Paterno to break Bear Bryant's all-time record for career coaching victories—and came very close to winning the other two (a 33–28 defeat at the hands of conference champion Illinois and a controversial 20–14 loss to Virginia).

Lions' Pride. With a little luck, 2002 would have been a King of Beasts year, but two midseason overtime losses (to Iowa and Michigan) prevented Paterno from enjoying another 11-win season. Penn State also lost to eventual national champion Ohio State (13–7) and to Auburn in the Outback Bowl (13–9), as its potent offense led by quarterback Zack Mills and running back Larry Johnson inexplicably lost its scoring punch. Nevertheless, Johnson became only the ninth player in NCAA Division I-A history (and the first in the history of the Big Ten Conference) to rush for more than 2,000 yards in the regular season. Johnson won the Maxwell and Walter Camp Player of the Year Awards as well as the Doak Walker Award, which is presented annually to the nation's top running back.

King of Beasts. Paterno thought he had all the necessary ingredients to complete his formula for excellence in 2002. Perhaps that is why his frustration level seemed particularly high during much of this season, especially with respect to consequential officiating errors that may have cost Penn State an opportunity to win at least 11 games and go to a major bowl.

Paterno's formula for excellence: two outstanding running backs and several dominating linebackers and defensive linemen. It is difficult to pinpoint the factors that kept the 2002 Lions from being crowned King of Beasts when they were just a few plays away from a perfect season. One vulnerability may have been the one-dimensional nature of the running game. Larry Johnson racked up an amazing 2,087 yards (a Penn State season record), but the next two leading ground gainers had only 263 and 201 yards, respectively—and they were both quarterbacks (Michael Robinson and Zack Mills)! The first defensive line of attack was awesome in 2002, with two of Penn State's four first-round NFL Draft picks playing at defensive tackle (Jimmy Kennedy) and defensive end (Michael Haynes). (The other first-rounders were Larry Johnson and wide receiver Bryant Johnson.) However, the Lions were somewhat vulnerable at linebacker and in the defensive backfield during the first half of the season, with costly results.

Cycle 11 (2003–2005): Five Decades of Excellence

Out of Whack. One of Paterno's least experienced teams ever showed promise on defense but struggled offensively throughout 2003, scoring 14 points or less in seven games and losing to 9 of its 12 opponents. Several different experiments were tried, but the bottom line was that the team was unable to rely on its inconsistent passing game to score points or on its offensive line to open holes for the running backs. Fortunately, success should be achievable in the future without having to make dramatic gains on offense, as the Lions lost only one game by more than two touchdowns in 2003.

Lions' Pride. Things will get better in 2004 as a young but very talented team continues to mature.

History would suggest that at least eight or nine wins can be expected. The key will be whether Paterno sticks to his formula for excellence and focuses on developing a ball-control running game and an opportunistic defense.

King of Beasts. It doesn't take a crystal ball to predict how Penn State will fare in 2005. All one needs is an understanding of Paterno's cycles of excellence to see that this could very well be the year when the greatest coach in the history of college football realizes his dream of having an undefeated team in five different decades—1968/1969, 1973, 1986, 1994, and, with any luck, 2005.

Paterno's formula for excellence: two outstanding running backs and several dominating linebackers and defensive linemen. Penn State has several promising young running backs who appear to be capable of big things, assuming a decent offensive line can be constructed from the new talent that has been recruited during the past two to three years. In particular, Austin Scott, the team's leading rusher in 2003, appears to be a good fit for Paterno's formula for excellence. Although it is not clear precisely who among the promising defensive underclassmen might achieve All-American status during the next two years, there are enough possibilities to excite even the most cynical fan. At linebacker, Paul Posluszny showed great potential toward the end of the 2003 season, and many are expecting his high school teammate, blue-chip recruit Dan Connor, to quickly move into a starring role. The defensive line performed erratically in 2003, but with a bit more consistency and experience, Tamba Hali and several underclassmen could become elite players.

The 100 Most Significant Games of the Paterno Era (1972–2003) and the Buttons That Tell Their Story

In the preceding pages, we provided an overview of both the tradition of Penn State football excellence under legendary coach Joe Paterno and the tradition of the buttons that have commemorated most of the games that Paterno has coached. In the following pages, we display the buttons associated with the 100 most significant games of the Paterno era since 1972 (when the button tradition began) while also providing pertinent game information, including date, location, attendance, and when the win or loss occurred in Paterno's coaching record. In addition, we briefly describe highlights of the game and why it was significant. We also offer an alternative "slogan that fits the story" that would have been appropriate had the outcome of the game been known in advance.

Of the 100 games selected by the authors, 25 were played during the 12 seasons since 1972 when the Nittany Lions were Out of Whack; 28 occurred during the 9 Lions' Pride seasons; and 47 were played during the 11 seasons when Penn State achieved King of Beasts status. All of Penn State's traditional Eastern opponents and every team in the Big Ten are represented, as are intersectional rivals from the SEC, ACC, Pac-10, Southwest Conference, and Mid-American Conference. About half of the 100 most significant games played during the Paterno era were against just eight teams: Ohio State (10), Pitt (8), Alabama (6), Notre Dame (6), Miami (5), Michigan (5), Michigan State (5), and Nebraska (4).

We hope you enjoy these particularly meaningful chapters in the Paterno legacy, as told through both the game stories and the button images linked to those stories.

JOE PATERNO'S TOP 100 GAMES

The Scores, the Buttons, the Stories

'97

Not a Pitty Picture

Ⓜ **Mellon Bank**

SEPTEMBER 6, 1997

UNIVERSITY PARK, PENNSYLVANIA

ATTENDANCE: 97,115

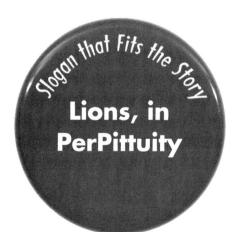

Slogan that Fits the Story

Lions, in PerPittuity

#100
Paterno Win 290

STORY LINE: Quarterback Mike McQueary shocks a defense focused on stopping the run by throwing for a school-record 366 yards and two touchdowns to wide receivers Joe Jurevicius and Joe Nastasi.

SIGNIFICANCE: PSU justifies its preseason No. 1 ranking with a convincing opening victory, while also reasserting its supremacy over archrival Pitt. Serious problems will emerge later in the season, but it's a great ride for Lion fans during September and October.

Season Record 9–3

#99
Paterno Loss
107

STORY LINE: An inspired Penn State squad proves it is better than its 2–6 record by taking a 20–14 lead deep into the fourth quarter against the defending national champions. The Buckeyes score the go-ahead touchdown with 1:35 remaining, but the Lions position themselves for a 60-yard field-goal try by long-kicking specialist David Kimball on the last play of the game. The kick is long enough but just wide.

NOVEMBER 1, 2003

UNIVERSITY PARK, PENNSYLVANIA

ATTENDANCE: 108,276

SIGNIFICANCE: One of Paterno's youngest teams ever gains confidence that it can return to elite status in 2004–2005.

Season Record 3–9

central counties bank says

Space Out Houston

cb

SEPTEMBER 17, 1977

UNIVERSITY PARK, PENNSYLVANIA

ATTENDANCE: 62,554

Slogan that Fits the Story

Houston, You Have a Problem

#98
Paterno Win 103

STORY LINE: In a reality test between highly ranked teams, quarterback Chuck Fusina leads a balanced offense to more than 500 yards while the defense continues to gel under the leadership of its new coordinator, Jerry Sandusky.

SIGNIFICANCE: After a steady three-year decline, PSU has a chance to show it is again ready to contend for a national title by defeating a respected intersectional opponent. This win sets the tone for a near-perfect season marred only by a four-point loss to Kentucky.

Season Record 11–1

PENN STATE 31 • HOUSTON 14

#97
Paterno Win 307

OUTBACK BOWL, JANUARY 1, 1999
Lion's Purrfection... Wildcat's Dejection
⓪ Mellon Bank
TAMPA, FLORIDA

STORY LINE: Kentucky quarterback and Heisman finalist Tim Couch passes for 336 yards, but the Lions' aggressive defense shuts down the Wildcats after giving up two early touchdowns. Defensive lineman Courtney Brown clinches the win with consecutive sacks to thwart a 17-play drive that would have brought the Wildcats within range.

SIGNIFICANCE: Penn State moves back into the top 20 in a productive but frustrating season in which their three losses were to the elite Big Ten teams they were hoping to replace.

JANUARY 1, 1999

TAMPA, FLORIDA, OUTBACK BOWL

ATTENDANCE: 66,005

Slogan that Fits the Story
Catnip for Lions

Season Record 9-3

central counties bank says '83 **Wrong Anther Panther** cb

NOVEMBER 19, 1983

PITTSBURGH, PENNSYLVANIA

ATTENDANCE: 60,283

Slogan that Fits the Story **Kibbles and Pitts**

#96
Paterno Tie 2

STORY LINE: After falling behind 21–10, the Panthers score twice to take the lead with 1:15 left in the game. The score is still 24–21 when the clock runs out, but the officials had earlier ordered that six seconds be added to compensate for an offside call, which leaves time for one more play.

SIGNIFICANCE: Paterno boldly calls for a fake from the 23-yard line, but Pitt calls a time-out and detects what Paterno has in mind. The Lions have no choice but to go for the tie.

Season Record 8-4-1

#95
Paterno Win 315

STORY LINE: Purdue holds the Lions to 11 first downs and outgains them by 126 yards, but long touchdown passes from quarterback Kevin Thompson to wide receivers Eddie Drummond and Chafie Fields, and two defensive touchdowns by defensive end Courtney Brown and linebacker Lavar Arrington, give PSU the edge in the only statistic that really matters.

SIGNIFICANCE: Penn State survives quarterback Drew Brees, but the offense's inconsistency and the defense's vulnerability to a precise ball-control passing game foreshadow future problems.

Season Record 10–3

'99
Much Purdue About Nothing
Mellon Bank

OCTOBER 23, 1999

WEST LAFAYETTE, INDIANA

ATTENDANCE: 68,355

Slogan that Fits the Story
Purdue No Harm

'01

It Isn't Easy Being Green

Mellon Bank

NOVEMBER 24, 2001

EAST LANSING, MICHIGAN

ATTENDANCE: 72,658

Slogan that Fits the Story

No Land Granted

#94
Paterno Win 327

STORY LINE: The Spartans take a 31–21 halftime lead, but the Lion defense makes the necessary adjustments and shuts down MSU quarterback Jeff Smoker. Running back Eric McCoo runs for three touchdowns and quarterback Zack Mills nails a 64-yard touchdown pass.

SIGNIFICANCE: The Lions retain the Land Grant Trophy for the seventh time in nine years and keep their bowl hopes alive with a clutch performance. The win makes Lion fans feel good about the recruiting decisions that brought Mills instead of Smoker to PSU.

Season Record 5–6

#93

Paterno Loss 55

STORY LINE: The Cavaliers are shut down after two first-half touchdown passes, but the Lion offense is repeatedly stymied and can manage only two field goals.

SIGNIFICANCE: The Lions lose their sixth game in the last seven and their first home opener in 24 years in what at the time appears to be a major upset. However, the game is not the disaster that some thought it was, as Virginia ends the season as the ACC champion and Penn State loses only two more games, one to No. 6 Alabama and one to No. 1 Notre Dame.

Season Record 8–3–1

No
Santa Here,
Virginia

Mellon Bank

SEPTEMBER 9, 1989

UNIVERSITY PARK, PENNSYLVANIA

ATTENDANCE: 85,956

Slogan that Fits the Story

Jeffersons Movin' on Up

No Roman Holiday

⓪ Mellon Bank

AUGUST 25, 1996

EAST RUTHERFORD, NEW JERSEY

ATTENDANCE: 77,716

Slogan that Fits the Story
Paterno Has Horse Sense

Paterno Win 279

STORY LINE: Running back Curtis Enis shrugs off Trojan tacklers as he piles up a near-record 241 yards and three touchdowns. The Lion defense opens eyes as USC, the defending Rose Bowl champs, are unable to get on the scoreboard until the last minute of the game—on an end zone fumble recovery.

SIGNIFICANCE: Hopes and expectations rise as the Lions appear to have the key elements needed for a Paterno championship team: a strong defense and a punishing running game.

Season Record 11–2

PENN STATE 24 • USC 7

#91
Paterno Win 332

STORY LINE: Running back Larry Johnson rushes for 257 yards, breaking Curt Warner's PSU single-game record by one yard. Quarterback Zack Mills and Larry's brother, wide receiver Tony Johnson, hook up for a 40-yard touchdown as both have big days.

SIGNIFICANCE: In 2001 the Lions needed a last-minute touchdown to pull out a 38–31 victory against the Wildcats and enable Paterno to tie Bear Bryant's all-time record of 323 wins. In this game, a rejuvenated defense enables PSU to score its first shutout in four seasons.

Season Record 9–4

OCTOBER 19, 2002

UNIVERSITY PARK, PENNSYLVANIA

ATTENDANCE: 108,853

It's Feudal: Knights

Mellon Bank

1984

#90
Paterno Win 171

SEPTEMBER 8, 1984

UNIVERSITY PARK, PENNSYLVANIA

ATTENDANCE: 84,409

STORY LINE: In a preview of offensive problems that will persist all season long, the Lions can manage only two field goals after running back D. J. Dozier runs for a touchdown on PSU's first possession, leaving it up to the defense to save the game.

SIGNIFICANCE: Former PSU assistant coach Dick Anderson almost pulls off the upset in his Scarlet Knight head coaching debut with his inside knowledge of Paterno's play calling. In the meantime, the "wave" is seen in Beaver Stadium for the first time.

Slogan that Fits the Story

Knights in White Flattened

Season Record 6–5

PENN STATE 15 • RUTGERS 12

45

#89
Paterno Loss 80

STORY LINE: A familiar pattern unfolds for the Lions. Though quite capable of pounding average teams, they cannot seem to make big defensive stops or cohesive drives against the three highly ranked foes on their schedule: Ohio State (No. 2), Michigan (No. 12), and Rose Bowl champion Wisconsin (No. 6).

SIGNIFICANCE: This disappointing loss illustrates how difficult it has been for even the best PSU teams to win more than six of eight Big Ten games, a feat accomplished only once so far (1994).

Season Record 9–3

'98
No Oscar for Madison
Mellon Bank

NOVEMBER 21, 1998

MADISON, WISCONSIN

ATTENDANCE: 78,964

Slogan that Fits the Story
Sometimes It's Easy Being Cheesy

Paterno Win 129

STORY LINE: North Carolina State scores with 1:18 to play to take a 7–6 lead. But 44 seconds later, with PSU facing fourth-and-24, quarterback Dayle Tate throws a 36-yard completion and kicker Herb Menhardt has an opportunity to try a 54-yard field goal. The kick is long enough but heads directly toward the right goal post! The ball hits the post and glances left and over the bar for the winning points.

SIGNIFICANCE: Penn State makes the most of an injury-filled season by pulling out a miracle victory against the Wolfpack on one of the most memorable plays in Nittany Lion history.

Season Record 8-4

NOVEMBER 10, 1979

RALEIGH, NORTH CAROLINA

ATTENDANCE: 51,200

PENN STATE 9 • N.C. STATE 7

#87

Paterno Win 225

STORY LINE: The PSU defense stuffs the run (six yards) and stifles the pass while racking up four sacks and five interceptions, two by safety Darren Perry.

SIGNIFICANCE: New Penn State President Joab Thomas, who was forced out of his job as Alabama president (in part for hiring a non-Alabaman as football coach), tells the Lions to "kick some butt." They do just that, proving they are one of the nation's top teams despite opening the season with close losses to Texas and USC.

Season Record 9–3

OCTOBER 27, 1990

BIRMINGHAM, ALABAMA

ATTENDANCE: 70,123

Bruise Syracuse

⑩ Mellon Bank

OCTOBER 17, 1987

SYRACUSE, NEW YORK

ATTENDANCE: 50,011

Slogan that Fits the Story

McPherson's Strutters

#86
Paterno Loss 46

STORY LINE: Coach MacPherson's Orangemen run up a 41–0 score, starting with quarterback Don McPherson's 80-yard bomb on the game's first play.

SIGNIFICANCE: PSU fans are incensed when the Nittany Lion shrine is painted orange, but they take comfort in the fact that this is only Paterno's second loss to Syracuse in 21 tries. The game is pivotal for the No. 10 ranked Lions, who enter the game at 5–1 but eventually disappear from the top 20 altogether.

Season Record 8–4

#85
Paterno Win 176

STORY LINE: PSU takes on another Heisman winner and again emerges with a win despite allowing quarterback Doug Flutie to pass for 447 yards. Big hits, five turnovers, and ball control by running back D. J. Dozier (143 yards) carry the day.

SIGNIFICANCE: The Lions enter the game with a shaky 5–3 record after a rare loss to West Virginia. With Notre Dame and Pitt still left to play, this game is critical to PSU's effort to preserve its record 45-year streak of nonlosing seasons.

Season Record 6–5

Hasbeans

Mellon Bank

1984

NOVEMBER 3, 1984

UNIVERSITY PARK, PENNSYLVANIA

ATTENDANCE: 85,690

Slogan that Fits the Story

Eagles Are Below Par

Knock Knock — Hoosier?

Mellon Bank

NOVEMBER 5, 1994

BLOOMINGTON, INDIANA

ATTENDANCE: 47,754

Slogan that Fits the Story

Indy Final Analysis — Lions

#84
Paterno Win 265

STORY LINE: With six minutes to go, running back Ki-Jana Carter runs for an 80-yard touchdown to open up a comfortable 35–14 lead. Indiana goes on to score 15 points against the Lion reserves, but in reality this is another blowout win.

SIGNIFICANCE: Legend has it that Indiana's furious finish cost the Lions a national championship, but PSU had already been dropped to No. 2 in the AP poll. Title-less Nebraska coach Tom Osborne was penciled in for No. 1 well before the Hoosiers showed up.

Season Record 12–0

#83
Paterno Loss 71

STORY LINE: Penn State opens up with 10 quick points, stagnates while OSU scores three touchdowns, and then comes back to take a 25–21 fourth-quarter lead on two solid drives led by quarterback Wally Richardson and running back Curtis Enis (146 yards). But in the end, the defense is unable to deny the powerful Buckeyes offense.

SIGNIFICANCE: The Lions fall to 0–2 in the conference with this loss, but rebound nicely to finish third in the Big Ten and only a couple of spots from another top 10 finish in the national polls.

OCTOBER 7, 1995

UNIVERSITY PARK, PENNSYLVANIA

ATTENDANCE: 96,655

Season Record 9–3

Slogan that Fits the Story

Too Much Buck Passing

central counties bank says

Slew Mizzou

cb

OCTOBER 4, 1980

COLUMBIA, MISSOURI

ATTENDANCE: 75,298

Slogan that Fits the Story

Lions Earn Their Stripes

#82
Paterno Win 134

STORY LINE: Penn State comes back from a 21–16 halftime deficit against the No. 9 Tigers. Cornerback Paul Lankford makes two crucial interceptions and freshman quarterback Todd Blackledge, making his first start after taking over for quarterback Jeff Hostetler (later a star at West Virginia), provides effective leadership.

SIGNIFICANCE: The Lions continue building the infrastructure for their great teams of 1981–1982 by adding Blackledge to an offense featuring running back Curt Warner and wide receiver Kenny Jackson.

Season Record 10–2

Paterno Win 84

STORY LINE: Linebacker Greg Buttle is accidentally knocked out by a pregame helmet throw from emotional running back Tom Donchez, but Buttle and his slow-starting teammates shut down overhyped Pitt running back Tony Dorsett. They eventually turn a 7–6 half-time deficit into a rout thanks to place-kicker Chris Bahr's four field goals.

SIGNIFICANCE: Penn State follows up a disappointing upset loss to North Carolina State with a resounding victory, thus preserving an opportunity for another 10-win season.

Season Record 10–2

NOVEMBER 28, 1974

PITTSBURGH, PENNSYLVANIA

ATTENDANCE: 48,895

PENN STATE 31 • PITT 10

'83

central counties bank says

Welcome To Everest

Paterno Win 167

STORY LINE: The 6–0 Mountaineers come into the game ranked No. 4 behind ex–PSU quarterback Jeff Hostetler, but West Virginia's defense is unable to contain running back Jon Williams (over 100 yards), quarterback Doug Strang (220 yards and three touchdown passes), or kick returner Kevin Baugh (punt return for a touchdown).

SIGNIFICANCE: The Lions follow their upset of No. 3 Alabama with another inspired performance against a ranked team, as Paterno continues his dominance (25–2) over the Mountaineers.

OCTOBER 22, 1983

UNIVERSITY PARK, PENNSYLVANIA

ATTENDANCE: 86,309

Slogan that Fits the Story

Nittany Is Too High

Season Record 8–4–1

PENN STATE 41 • WEST VIRGINIA 23

Paterno Loss
35

STORY LINE: Nebraska seeks revenge with one of its most powerful teams ever—and gets it. New PSU quarterbacks Doug Strang and Don Lonergan are unable to establish any offensive continuity, and the defense is overwhelmed.

SIGNIFICANCE: The Cornhuskers set the tone for the season as the Lions open with three straight losses for the first time in Paterno's career. An infusion of young talent will eventually stop the bleeding, but at this point 1983 has become a rebuilding year.

AUGUST 29, 1983

EAST RUTHERFORD, NEW JERSEY

ATTENDANCE: 71,123

Season Record 8-4-1

PENN STATE 6 • NEBRASKA 44

Paterno Win 295

STORY LINE: One of the worst-played PSU games in history turns into one of their most fantastic victories as the Lions come back from a 15–3 fourth-quarter deficit. With the clock ticking down, they launch a long touchdown drive. They then survive what could have been their last opportunity by forcing a fumble deep in Minnesota territory and scoring the winning touchdown on the next play.

SIGNIFICANCE: Running back Aaron Harris suffers a season-ending knee injury, and the No. 1 Lions are never the same.

Season Record 9–3

OCTOBER 18, 1997

UNIVERSITY PARK, PENNSYLVANIA

ATTENDANCE: 96,953

PENN STATE 16 • MINNESOTA 15

#77
Paterno Win 91

STORY LINE: West Virginia enters the game with the nation's fourth-best scoring offense but is held to under 200 yards by a dominating defense. The Lion offense also excels, though in six other games it is unable to score more than 15 points.

SIGNIFICANCE: Had Mountaineers coach (later Florida State coach) Bobby Bowden won just a couple of his battles with PSU during his six years with the team (1970–1975), Paterno (6–1 versus Bowden) might never have become the winningest coach in major college football in 2001–2002.

Season Record 9–3

OCTOBER 11, 1975

UNIVERSITY PARK, PENNSYLVANIA

ATTENDANCE: 59,658

No Safe Harbor in Ann Arbor

Mellon Bank

NOVEMBER 16, 1996

ANN ARBOR, MICHIGAN

ATTENDANCE: 105,898

Slogan that Fits the Story

Pop Goes the Weasel

#76
Paterno Win 287

STORY LINE: Penn State wins in classic Paterno style, breaking open a tight game in the second half with a blocked punt by cornerback David Macklin that linebacker Ahmad Collins runs in for the score. They then seal the deal by relying on turnovers from an opportunistic defense led by safety Kim Herring.

SIGNIFICANCE: The Lions beat Michigan for the third time in a row, a feat unmatched in 30 years. PSU has lost the last six matchups (1997–2002), but we are confident that streak will end in 2005.

Season Record 11–2

PENN STATE 29 • MICHIGAN 17

#75
Paterno Loss 109

STORY LINE: The Lions expected better after clobbering Indiana 52–7, but they suffer all kinds of miscues and mistakes to hand the Spartans an easy win.

SIGNIFICANCE: Penn State finishes with nine losses for the first time in its long and storied history, a result that can be attributed to the fact that the 1999 recruiting class was the smallest ever during the Paterno era and 2003 was a predictable down year after sending four first-round draft picks to the NFL. The potential for excellence in 2004 and 2005 remains.

Season Record 3–9

NOVEMBER 22, 2003

EAST LANSING, MICHIGAN

ATTENDANCE: 72,119

Slogan that Fits the Story
Faux Pas for Joepa

60

JANUARY 1, 1996

TAMPA, FLORIDA,
OUTBACK BOWL

ATTENDANCE: 65,313

#74
Paterno Win 278

STORY LINE: After a slow start (three field goals from place-kicker Brett Conway), the Lion offense adjusts to the muddy, rainy conditions with four touchdown passes from quarterback Wally Richardson, including two to wide receiver and Biletnikoff Award–winner Bobby Engram.

SIGNIFICANCE: Running back Brian Milne, who overcame cancer to become one of PSU's greatest fullbacks, has his most productive rushing day in his final game. It is his best contest since scoring the winning touchdown at the end of "The Drive" in the legendary 1994 Illinois game.

Season Record 9–3

#73
Paterno Win 143

STORY LINE: Nebraska plays tough at home, but the Lions are even more productive. They overcome a 24–20 fourth-quarter deficit behind running back Curt Warner's 238 yards and place kicker Brian Franco's record-setting five field goals.

SIGNIFICANCE: The Lions go overboard upgrading their schedule, as this game is followed by Miami, new foes Alabama and Notre Dame, and No. 1 Pitt. Although PSU wins only three of these five games, the relentless schedule prepares the team well for its 1982 title run.

Season Record 10–2

central counties bank says

Nittany Crack Corn

cb

SEPTEMBER 26, 1981

LINCOLN, NEBRASKA

ATTENDANCE: 76,308

Slogan that Fits the Story

Kernel Klink

#72
Paterno Loss 19

SEPTEMBER 18, 1976

UNIVERSITY PARK, PENNSYLVANIA

ATTENDANCE: 62,503

STORY LINE: The unlucky Lions might have won this game against the top-ranked Buckeyes if not for two turnovers inside their opponent's 10-yard line. Ohio State plays a mistake-free game and holds on for the victory.

SIGNIFICANCE: The Ohio State defeat is a turning point, as it leads to the first three-game losing streak of Paterno's career. On a more positive note, the subsequent infusion of new talent into the lineup helps make 1976 a successful rebuilding year.

Season Record
7–5

PENN STATE 7 • OHIO STATE 12

#71
Paterno Win 85

STORY LINE: The Lions repeat their season-long habit of laying low in the first half (7–3 deficit). They then rack up several quick scores behind quarterback Tom Shuman, running back Tom Donchez, wide receiver Jimmy Cefalo, kicker Chris Bahr, and wide receiver Joe Jackson's alert 50-yard touchdown runback of an onside kick.

SIGNIFICANCE: The powerful Lions, despite their tendency to hibernate from time to time, outlast the Cinderella Bears to finish in the top 10 for the seventh time in eight years.

Season Record 10–2

JANUARY 1, 1975

DALLAS, TEXAS, COTTON BOWL

ATTENDANCE: 67,500

Lion Eyes are Smilin'

Mellon Bank

NOVEMBER 16, 1991

UNIVERSITY PARK, PENNSYLVANIA

ATTENDANCE: 96,672

Slogan that Fits the Story

Bend South, Irish

#70
Paterno Win 238

STORY LINE: PSU storms out to a 21–0 first-quarter lead and cruises from there, as wide receiver O. J. McDuffie and running back Richie Anderson have huge days. The defense also comes up big with a key goal-line stand in the second quarter.

SIGNIFICANCE: The Lions earn another Fiesta Bowl invitation with this win. They also serve notice that, despite a couple of earlier losses (to USC and Miami), they have developed into one of the most powerful and well-balanced teams of the Paterno era.

Season Record 11–2

#69
Paterno Win 286

Lions —
King Among
Cats

Ⓜ Mellon Bank

STORY LINE: A determined PSU squad scores on its first two drives and races out to a big halftime lead while crushing Northwestern with seven sacks and three interceptions. The offense shows great balance with 201 yards passing from quarterback Wally Richardson and 167 yards rushing from running back Curtis Enis.

SIGNIFICANCE: This is a critical game in a season that was in danger of slipping away after an upset loss to Iowa. The Lions reaffirm their destiny with a huge win over the No. 10 ranked Wildcats.

NOVEMBER 2, 1996

UNIVERSITY PARK, PENNSYLVANIA

ATTENDANCE: 96,596

Slogan that Fits the Story

Shrinking Violets

Season Record 11–2

Troy Troy Again

⟋⟍ **Mellon Bank**

SEPTEMBER 10, 1994

UNIVERSITY PARK, PENNSYLVANIA

ATTENDANCE: 96,463

Slogan that Fits the Story

Southern Cal's on Shaky Ground

#68
Paterno Win 259

STORY LINE: The Lions score twice in the first two minutes and effortlessly run up a 35–0 halftime lead, as wide receiver Freddie Scott, running back Ki-Jana Carter, and tight end Kyle Brady make one big play after another.

SIGNIFICANCE: After an opening 56–3 win at Minnesota in which the Lions' perfectly balanced offense gained nearly 700 yards (345 rushing and 344 passing), PSU shows it is capable of destroying highly ranked opponents as well, racking up more than 500 yards of total offense.

Season Record 12–0

PENN STATE 38 • USC 14

#67
Paterno Loss 60

STORY LINE: In a frustrating game filled with mistakes, Penn State squanders several scoring opportunities with turnovers and dropped passes. Backup quarterback Tom Bill rallies the Lions in the fourth quarter but can't close a 14-point gap.

SIGNIFICANCE: After a series of losses to PSU while coaching at West Virginia, Florida State coach Bobby Bowden finally gets the best of Joe Paterno in the inaugural Blockbuster Bowl. Penn State nevertheless finishes in the top 10 (coaches poll) for the first time in four years.

Season Record 9–3

Ambushed–
Lion Style

Mellon Bank

BLOCKBUSTER BOWL • DECEMBER 28, 1990

DECEMBER 28, 1990

MIAMI, FLORIDA,
BLOCKBUSTER BOWL

ATTENDANCE: 74,021

Slogan that Fits the Story

Nole
Contendre

68

NOVEMBER 21, 1981

UNIVERSITY PARK,
PENNSYLVANIA

ATTENDANCE: 84,175

#66
Paterno Win 149

STORY LINE: The Lions rebound from a loss to an inspired Alabama squad to give Paterno his first of eight wins (versus five losses) against the Irish. A big goal-line stand and a crucial interception by defensive tackle Gary Gattuso set up the winning drive, as the Lions come back from a 21–17 deficit late in the fourth quarter.

SIGNIFICANCE: Penn State's ability to handle adversity is severely tested in several games in 1981, helping to create one of Paterno's most resilient teams ever in 1982.

Season Record 10–2

Paterno Win 111

STORY LINE: Pitt quarterback Matt Cavanaugh survives five sacks and three picks to launch a dramatic touchdown drive in the game's final minute, but defensive tackle Matt Millen and company stuff the two-point conversion attempt to hold off the No. 10 Panthers.

SIGNIFICANCE: Penn State wraps up a near-perfect season but misses out on a major bowl bid. The Lions go on to defeat Arizona State in Paterno's first of six Fiesta Bowl wins, as they finish the season ranked in the top 5 for the first time since 1973.

NOVEMBER 26, 1977

PITTSBURGH, PENNSYLVANIA

ATTENDANCE: 56,500

Season Record 11–1

PENN STATE 15 • PITT 13

Central counties bank says
Temple, Whoo?
cb

SEPTEMBER 1, 1978

PHILADELPHIA,
PENNSYLVANIA

ATTENDANCE: 53,103

Slogan that Fits the Story
Joe Is
Owl
Knowing

#64
Paterno Win
113

STORY LINE: An impenetrable PSU defense gives up only 126 yards, but the Owls almost pull off the upset by regularly punting on third down for field position. Place-kicker Matt Bahr boots the winning field goal in the game's waning seconds.

SIGNIFICANCE: The Lions encounter some powerhouse teams in 1978 on the road to No. 1, but it is the lightly regarded Owls who come the closest to depriving the Nittany Lions of an undefeated regular season and a chance to play for the national championship.

Season Record
11–1

#63
Paterno Win 165

STORY LINE: The 2–3 Lions take on third-ranked Alabama in what is expected to be a rout. For three quarters it *is* a rout as PSU takes a shocking 34–7 lead after forcing six turnovers. However, three late touchdowns bring Alabama back to 34–28, and, with nine seconds to go, they are poised to score again.

SIGNIFICANCE: The Lions pull off a truly fantastic finish as a controversial incompletion that is very close to being the winning touchdown is followed by a defensive stop on the 1-yard line.

Season Record 8–4–1

central counties bank says '83
'Terno The Tide
db

OCTOBER 8, 1983

UNIVERSITY PARK, PENNSYLVANIA

ATTENDANCE: 85,614

Slogan that Fits the Story
Lions Slamma Bama

#62
Paterno Loss 14

STORY LINE: PSU outgains Navy by 378 to 172 total yards, but the Midshipmen, coached by former Lion assistant coach George Welsh, are better able to navigate a driving rainstorm. The Lions miss several field goals, lose five fumbles, and fail on a fourth-quarter two-point conversion attempt.

SIGNIFICANCE: This stunning upset—possibly the biggest of the Paterno era—transforms what might have been another run at a national championship into a season of "what if" scenarios.

SEPTEMBER 21, 1974

UNIVERSITY PARK, PENNSYLVANIA

ATTENDANCE: 42,000

Season Record 10–2

PENN STATE 6 · NAVY 7

#61
Paterno Win 197

STORY LINE: Notre Dame quarterback Steve Beuerlein passes for 311 yards and positions the Irish for the winning score in the final minute. But a heroic goal-line stand led by safety Ray Isom and defensive end Bob White clinches the win.

SIGNIFICANCE: After watching PSU narrowly beat Maryland the previous week (by knocking down a last-second two-point conversion pass), new Notre Dame coach Lou Holtz figures he can upset the 9–0 Lions as he had a couple of times as coach of North Carolina State. Sorry, Lou.

NOVEMBER 15, 1986

SOUTH BEND, INDIANA

ATTENDANCE: 59,075

Season Record 12–0

74

Central counties bank says Scatter the Pack

NOVEMBER 6, 1976

UNIVERSITY PARK,
PENNSYLVANIA

ATTENDANCE: 60,426

Slogan that Fits the Story

Big Numbers for Joe

#60
Paterno Win 100

STORY LINE: An opportunistic Lion defense forces six turnovers while the offense gains 530 yards in its most productive outing of the season. Running backs Steve Geise and Mike Guman each rush for more than 100 yards.

SIGNIFICANCE: Despite an early-season losing streak and a season-ending slump that ensured this would not be one of Penn State's better seasons, the Lions play an inspired game when they have a chance to help Paterno earn his 100th victory as a head coach.

Season Record 7–5

PENN STATE 41 • N.C. STATE 20

#59

Paterno Win 277

Big
MichStake

Ⓜ Mellon Bank

STORY LINE: With two minutes left to play and trailing 20–17, PSU elects to punt, hoping to stop the Spartans and get one last scoring opportunity. The defense does its job and quarterback Wally Richardson takes over, throwing 12 straight passes to move the Lions to the 4-yard line. Wide receiver Bobby Engram looks like an escape artist as he takes a middle screen pass and dives for the touchdown.

SIGNIFICANCE: Engram saves the game and the season for the Lions, who might have been 5–7 without him.

NOVEMBER 25, 1995

EAST LANSING, MICHIGAN

ATTENDANCE: 66,189

Season Record 9–3

Slogan that Fits the Story

Easy Green to Read

It's Pay
Buck Time

Mellon Bank

OCTOBER 5, 1996

COLUMBUS, OHIO

ATTENDANCE: 94,241

Slogan that Fits the Story

Like a
Million
Bucks

#58
Paterno Loss
73

STORY LINE: After four blowout victories and a big win over undefeated Wisconsin (PSU's 700th football win), the time has come for Penn State to prove it is worthy of its No. 3 ranking. However, this time it is the Lions who are blown away, as No. 4 OSU pounds out 565 (versus 211) yards of total offense.

SIGNIFICANCE: Suspicions that the 1996 Lions might need more time to mature are confirmed in this early season battle, although the experience pays off as PSU later manhandles three ranked teams.

Season Record
11–2

#57
Paterno Win 257

STORY LINE: Tennessee zips out to an early 10–0 lead behind star quarterback Heath Shuler, but an intimidating defense torments Shuler and his receivers the rest of the game while the Lions' balanced offense runs up the score.

SIGNIFICANCE: The No. 5 Volunteers come into the game as heavy favorites but are swatted away by a versatile offense that soon will become one of the greatest in PSU and NCAA history. Paterno's 15th bowl victory ties him with Bear Bryant for most career bowl wins.

Season Record 10–2

CompUSA Florida Citrus Bowl
Don't Volunteer for Lion Duty
Ⓜ **Mellon Bank**
JANUARY 1, 1994

JANUARY 1, 1994

ORLANDO, FLORIDA, CITRUS BOWL

ATTENDANCE: 72,456

Slogan that Fits the Story
Heath Bar Crunch

NOVEMBER 16, 2002

BLOOMINGTON, INDIANA

ATTENDANCE: 27,454

Slogan that Fits the Story

Speed Trap for Indy

#56
Paterno Win 335

STORY LINE: Running back Larry Johnson scores four touchdowns while rushing for a prodigious 327 yards on just 28 carries. Cornerback Rich Gardner chips in with an interception for a touchdown while linebacker Derek Wake and cornerback Anwar Phillips also star.

SIGNIFICANCE: Paterno extends his perfect record against Indiana to 8–0 while LJ does what running backs John Cappelletti, Curt Warner, Ki-Jana Carter, and many others could not do: break Lydell Mitchell's PSU record of 1,567 yards rushing in a season.

Season Record 9–4

PENN STATE 58 • INDIANA 25

#55

Paterno Loss
85

STORY LINE: The Rockets zoom out to a 24–0 lead and cruise the rest of the way with a ball-control offense that eats up more than 40 minutes of possession time. The only Penn State highlight is a 61-yard touchdown pass from quarterback Rashard Casey to running back Larry Johnson.

SIGNIFICANCE: Losing to USC in the opener is worrisome, but this convincing defeat to a Mid-American Conference team makes Paterno's second losing season in 35 years seem inevitable.

Season Record
5–7

SEPTEMBER 2, 2000

UNIVERSITY PARK, PENNSYLVANIA

ATTENDANCE: 94,296

Slogan that Fits the Story
Your Song, Rocket Man

Buzz Off!

Ⓜ **Mellon Bank**

AUGUST 28, 1991

EAST RUTHERFORD, NEW JERSEY

ATTENDANCE: 77,409

Slogan that Fits the Story

Sting Operation for Lions

#54
Paterno Win 230

STORY LINE: The Lions crush the Yellowjackets behind an opportunistic defense (four turnovers) and quarterback Tony Sacca's record-setting five touchdowns, including a spectacular 39-yard touchdown catch by wide receiver O. J. McDuffie that he grabs after the pass is broken up and he is lying on the ground.

SIGNIFICANCE: Paterno knows he has one of his best teams ever, but almost everyone else is shocked to see the Nittany Lions run up a 34–3 lead on the defending national champions.

Season Record 11–2

PENN STATE 34 · GEORGIA TECH 22

#53
Paterno Win
308

'99

Errorzona

Ⓜ Mellon Bank

STORY LINE: Penn State runs up a 31–0 halftime lead on explosive scoring plays by wide receiver Chafie Fields, running back Larry Johnson, and running back Aaron Harris as the offense accumulates more than 500 yards of total offense. In the meantime, the highly ranked Wildcats are shut out until the last minute of the game.

SIGNIFICANCE: Right on schedule, the 1999 Lions establish themselves as serious contenders for a national title with a strategic big-play defense and a balanced big-play offense.

AUGUST 28, 1999

UNIVERSITY PARK, PENNSYLVANIA

ATTENDANCE: 97,168

Season Record 10–3

Slogan that Fits the Story

Razing Arizona

'01

Get Reel,
Virginia

⟨⟨⟨ Mellon Bank

DECEMBER 1, 2001

CHARLOTTESVILLE,
VIRGINIA

ATTENDANCE: 57,005

Slogan that Fits the Story

Charlottesville's Web

#52
Paterno Loss 96

STORY LINE: With PSU leading 14–6 and closing in on another score, the Cavaliers return a "fumble" 92 yards for a touchdown that should not have counted. The deflated Lions make too many mistakes after that to come back.

SIGNIFICANCE: After a tough 0–4 start that might have been avoided if this game had been played as scheduled on the weekend after 9/11, the Lions win five of six games and are poised to go to a bowl game. Instead, Paterno suffers his third losing season in 36 years.

Season Record 5–6

#51
Paterno Win 276

STORY LINE: The Lions manage to hold on to a slim lead entering the fourth quarter, but it is still anybody's game as Penn State lines up for a field-goal attempt from the 2-yard line that would expand their lead to 23–17. But it's a fake! Holder Joe Nastasi runs over right tackle to put the game out of reach.

SIGNIFICANCE: A 17-inch snowfall three days before the game disrupts the region, but a heroic snow-removal effort makes it possible for dedicated fans to watch a very entertaining game.

Season Record 9–3

Michigan Impossible

Mellon Bank

NOVEMBER 18, 1995

UNIVERSITY PARK, PENNSYLVANIA

ATTENDANCE: 80,000

Slogan that Fits the Story

Snowball's Chance at Best

Plaster Pitt

CENTRAL COUNTIES BANK SAYS

NOVEMBER 24, 1973

UNIVERSITY PARK, PENNSYLVANIA

ATTENDANCE: 56,600

Slogan that Fits the Story

Chompin' at the Pitt

#50
Paterno Win 74

STORY LINE: Pitt takes a 13–3 lead but angers the dozing Lions when kicker Carson Long shakes his fist at the PSU bench after nailing a 51-yard field goal to close out the half. The Lion offense explodes while an aroused defense stuffs the Panthers.

SIGNIFICANCE: The Lions complete another undefeated season in style, with running back John Cappelletti outgaining Pitt running back Tony Dorsett 161 to 77 and finishing the season as Penn State's number two all-time rusher (with 1,522 yards) behind the great Lydell Mitchell (1,567 yards).

Season Record 12–0

#49
Paterno Loss
62

STORY LINE: Miami breaks open a tight game with two huge plays: an 80-yard touchdown pass and a 91-yard punt return. The Lions fight back behind quarterback Tony Sacca but are unable to come up with one last big play.

SIGNIFICANCE: This is a peak year in Paterno's cycle of excellence, but this defeat (after an earlier loss to USC) makes it virtually impossible to move back into title contention. The Lions finish with a No. 3 ranking, but inconsistency costs them a shot at No. 1.

Season Record
11–2

Storm's Over

⑩ Mellon Bank

OCTOBER 12, 1991

MIAMI, FLORIDA

ATTENDANCE: 75,723

Slogan that Fits the Story

Canes Are Able

FIESTA BOWL, JANUARY 1, 1997

PSU Fiesta- Texas Siesta

Mellon Bank

TEMPE, ARIZONA

JANUARY 1, 1997

TEMPE, ARIZONA, FIESTA BOWL

ATTENDANCE: 65,106

Slogan that Fits the Story

Bum Steers

#48
Paterno Win 289

STORY LINE: The Longhorns dominate for 30 minutes and take a 12–7 halftime lead. But Kenny Watson returns the second-half kickoff 81 yards to set up the go-ahead touchdown, and wide receiver Chafie Fields sets up another on an 84-yard reverse as the Lions rack up 330 yards of total offense in the final two quarters.

SIGNIFICANCE: Coach Paterno celebrates his 70th birthday with his fourth straight bowl win (Citrus, Rose, Outback, and Fiesta) and his sixth Fiesta Bowl win in six tries.

Season Record 11–2

PENN STATE 38 • TEXAS 15

#47
Paterno Loss 98

STORY LINE: The Lions' last-minute drive for the go-ahead score is thwarted by a bad call as a completed pass is ruled out of bounds. In overtime, Michigan follows a PSU field goal with the winning touchdown despite 264 yards passing by quarterback Zack Mills.

SIGNIFICANCE: Penn State experiences one of its most painful losses ever—its second overtime loss of the year—in a superbly played game that neither team should have lost. The game sets the pattern for 2002: close to greatness but just a play short here and there.

*Season Record
9–4*

'02

Lions, Bring
Down The
Big House

◆ CITIZENS BANK

OCTOBER 12, 2002

ANN ARBOR, MICHIGAN

ATTENDANCE: 111,502

Slogan that Fits the Story

**Mich
Trial**

Irish Eyes Are Crying
Mellon Bank

NOVEMBER 21, 1987

UNIVERSITY PARK, PENNSYLVANIA

ATTENDANCE: 84,000

Slogan that Fits the Story

No Gold Here, Irish

#46
Paterno Win 207

STORY LINE: Blair Thomas has his best day rushing (214 yards) in an evenly matched game in which both teams gain 312 yards. Notre Dame goes for the win after scoring in the final minute, but defensive tackle Pete Curkendall and linebacker Keith Karpinski are there to stop Notre Dame quarterback Tony Rice on the option keeper.

SIGNIFICANCE: The Lions, 7–3 after a shutout loss to Pitt, make the most of an inconsistent season by finishing with a glorious upset victory over the seventh-ranked Irish and coach Lou Holtz.

Season Record 8-4

PENN STATE 21 • NOTRE DAME 20

#45
Paterno Win 141

STORY LINE: Running back Curt Warner scores on a 64-yard jaunt on the Lions' first offensive play, but OSU takes a 19–10 lead as quarterback Art Schlichter racks up 244 yards passing in the first half. The second half is a different story, as the defense holds the Buckeyes to zero yards in the third quarter.

SIGNIFICANCE: The Lion coaching staff is right on target with its halftime adjustments, as PSU rebounds from a tough loss to Pitt to finish in the top 10 for the 11th time in 14 years.

Season Record 10–2

central counties bank says
Bye-Bye Buckeyes

DECEMBER 26, 1980

TEMPE, ARIZONA, FIESTA BOWL

ATTENDANCE: 66,738

Slogan that Fits the Story
Beat PSU? They're Nuts

Floor Da Canes

central counties bank says

#44
Paterno Loss 32

STORY LINE: The Lions cannot overcome four turnovers, four missed field goals, running back Curt Warner's early departure due to a hamstring injury, or a driving rainstorm despite quarterback Todd Blackledge's heroic late-game comeback effort.

SIGNIFICANCE: This self-inflicted loss is one of the most frustrating of Paterno's career, as he had assembled a team with legitimate title aspirations that had risen to No. 1 after six big wins. JoePa's quest for a consensus national championship would have to wait one more year.

OCTOBER 31, 1981

MIAMI, FLORIDA

ATTENDANCE: 32,117

Slogan that Fits the Story

Perfect Storm

Season Record 10–2

PENN STATE 14 • MIAMI 17

#43
Paterno Win 316

STORY LINE: A dominating defense sets the tone for the 9–0 Lions, as defensive end Courtney Brown sets a new PSU career sack record and linebacker Lavar Arrington makes what is widely regarded as the defensive play of the year.

SIGNIFICANCE: This game will forever be remembered for the extraordinary "Lavar Leap," a fourth-down stop of an Illini running back in which Lavar, with perfect timing, launches himself over the line and stuffs the ball carrier for a three-yard loss just as he is handed the ball.

Season Record 10–3

'98

Silence The 'Nois

Ⓜ **Mellon Bank**

OCTOBER 31, 1998

UNIVERSITY PARK, PENNSYLVANIA

ATTENDANCE: 96,508

Slogan that Fits the Story

Champaign Bash for Lavar

SEPTEMBER 14, 2002

UNIVERSITY PARK,
PENNSYLVANIA

ATTENDANCE: 110,753

Slogan that Fits the Story

Creamed Corn

#42
Paterno Win 329

STORY LINE: The entire team comes up big as cornerback Rich Gardner scores on an interception return and quarterback Zack Mills and running back Larry Johnson combine for almost 400 yards. Backup quarterback Michael Robinson adds to the fun with two touchdowns.

SIGNIFICANCE: PSU hands the seventh-ranked Cornhuskers their worst loss in 12 years in a statement game: after two losing seasons, Paterno's rebuilding efforts are succeeding and he is ready to move the Lions back to national prominence.

Season Record 9–4

#41
Paterno Win 106

STORY LINE: The Lions cruise for three quarters with quarterback Chuck Fusina at the helm, but then have to hang on as Syracuse quarterback Bill Hurley rallies the Orangemen with a record-setting passing performance.

SIGNIFICANCE: Paterno misses the only game of his head coaching career to be with his son David, who had been hospitalized the previous day after suffering a fractured skull in a trampoline accident. The Lions do not look sharp in his absence.

Season Record 11–1

central counties bank says
Grind the Rind

cb

OCTOBER 15, 1977

SYRACUSE, NEW YORK

ATTENDANCE: 27,029

Slogan that Fits the Story
Orangemen, and Joe, Are Blue

NOVEMBER 27, 1993

EAST LANSING, MICHIGAN

ATTENDANCE: 85,690

#40
Paterno Win
256

STORY LINE: The huge MSU offensive line pushes the Lions around for three quarters and rolls up what appears to be an insurmountable 37–17 lead. But cornerback Derek Bochna's interception ignites an amazing five-minute offensive eruption that foreshadows the undefeated 1994 season, as quarterback Kerry Collins throws for 352 yards and three touchdowns, including two on long bombs to wide receiver Bobby Engram.

SIGNIFICANCE: The Lions earn a spot in the Citrus Bowl with one of the greatest comeback wins in PSU history.

Season Record
10–2

#39

Paterno Win 200

STORY LINE: The Falcons take a 7–3 lead at the end of the first quarter, but the Lions then take charge as both the defense (linebacker Quintus McDonald) and special teams (kick returner Ray Roundtree) add to the scoring outburst.

SIGNIFICANCE: Coach Paterno earns his 200th victory in his first game after being named *Sports Illustrated's* "Sportsman of the Year." In an odd coincidence, the only other game between PSU and Bowling Green happens to be Paterno's 300th coaching victory.

Season Record 8-4

Lions Bowling Party

Ⓜ Mellon Bank

SEPTEMBER 5, 1987

UNIVERSITY PARK, PENNSYLVANIA

ATTENDANCE: 84,574

Slogan that Fits the Story

Not in This Millennium, Falcon

SEPTEMBER 4, 1993

UNIVERSITY PARK, PENNSYLVANIA

ATTENDANCE: 95,387

#38
Paterno Win 248

STORY LINE: Wide receiver Bobby Engram, out the previous year after some legal trouble, scores on a 29-yard screen pass on the Lions' first offensive play and adds three more touchdown catches to break the all-time PSU touchdown reception record. Quarterback John Sacca and running back Ki-Jana Carter lead an offense that gains more than 500 yards.

SIGNIFICANCE: PSU's Big Ten debut is a smashing success, as fans enjoy watching Sacca and Gopher quarterback Tim Schade combine for 98 passes, with 4 of Schade's 66 passes caught by PSU defenders.

Season Record 10–2

#37

Paterno Win 177

STORY LINE: Safety Mike Zordich returns an interception for a touchdown on the second play of the game to jump-start a 17-point run, but Maryland fights back to go ahead 18–17. PSU kicks a field goal and then hangs on as the Terrapins miss two late field-goal tries and fumble away a chance to win in the final minute.

SIGNIFICANCE: Maryland still can't beat Paterno despite its No. 1 preseason rating by *Sports Illustrated*. Zordich's play sets the tone for a season dominated by big plays on defense and special teams.

Season Record 11–1

SEPTEMBER 7, 1985

COLLEGE PARK, MARYLAND

ATTENDANCE: 50,750

'97
**Driving
Mich
Crazy**

///) Mellon Bank

NOVEMBER 9, 1997

**UNIVERSITY PARK,
PENNSYLVANIA**

ATTENDANCE: 97,498

Slogan that Fits the Story
**High Crimes
and
Michdemeanors**

#36
Paterno Loss
75

STORY LINE: The eventual national champion nails Penn State with its first loss of the season by capitalizing on the Lions' mistakes and playing a nearly perfect game from beginning to end.

SIGNIFICANCE: PSU's weaknesses are exploited by one of Michigan's best teams ever. The Lions are also embarrassed at season's end by MSU, Florida, and two key players: running back Curtis Enis (lying about contact with a sports agent) and wide receiver Joe Jurevicius (academic eligibility).

*Season Record
9–3*

Paterno Win 250

STORY LINE: A dominating Penn State defense turns in nine sacks and three interceptions and does not allow the Hawkeyes to cross midfield in the second half. Running back Ki-Jana Carter runs for more than 100 yards for the third straight game.

SIGNIFICANCE: Paterno's 250th win is one of the greatest defensive games in Penn State history, but a controversy erupts on offense when backup quarterback Kerry Collins takes over for quarterback John Sacca. Two weeks later Sacca shocks Lion fans by leaving the team.

Season Record 10–2

All Hawk and No Action

Mellon Bank

SEPTEMBER 18, 1993

IOWA CITY, IOWA

ATTENDANCE: 70,397

Slogan that Fits the Story

They're Just Kitty Hawks

PENN STATE 31 • IOWA 0

JANUARY 1, 1982

TEMPE, ARIZONA,
FIESTA BOWL

ATTENDANCE: 71,053

#34
Paterno Win 151

STORY LINE: USC running back and Heisman winner Marcus Allen (85 yards, no touchdowns) fumbles on the game's first play, and PSU All-American running back Curt Warner (145 yards, two touchdowns) scores two plays later. The Lions cruise to an easy victory with an all-around team effort, including a blocked punt for a safety.

SIGNIFICANCE: The Lions jump to No. 3 in the polls—and No. 1 in the Sagarin Ratings and Dunkel System—after finishing the year looking as strong as any team in the country. Their brutal schedule included six top 20 teams.

Season Record 11–1

PENN STATE 26 • USC 10

#33
Paterno Win 263

Sleepless in
Ann Arbor

Mellon Bank

STORY LINE: The Lions jump out to a 16–0 advantage, but the Wolverines fight back, and with five minutes to play the game is tied at 24. PSU confidently clinches the win on a touchdown pass (quarterback Kerry Collins' third) to wide receiver Bobby Engram. A diving interception by cornerback Brian Miller kills Michigan's last-gasp drive.

SIGNIFICANCE: In 1993 Michigan upset a 5–0 PSU team with serious title aspirations, 21–13. In 1994 the 5–0 Lions turn the tables, beating their toughest rival in the Big House.

OCTOBER 15, 1994

ANN ARBOR, MICHIGAN

ATTENDANCE: 106,832

Season Record 12–0

Slogan that Fits the Story

Mich
M*A*S*H

Ride the Tide
Mellon Bank

OCTOBER 12, 1985

UNIVERSITY PARK, PENNSYLVANIA

ATTENDANCE: 85,444

Slogan that Fits the Story
Tidy Work, Lions

#32
Paterno Win 181

STORY LINE: Thanks to four field goals from Massimo Manca, Penn State nurses a 12–10 lead into the fourth quarter. A clutch drive highlighted by quarterback Matt Knizner's bootleg touchdown pass to tight end Brian Siverling clinches the win.

SIGNIFICANCE: This is the defining game of an amazing streak in which the Lions win by a touchdown or less in seven of their first eight games while never scoring more than 27 points. PSU finishes big against Notre Dame and Pitt to give Paterno his fifth undefeated regular season.

Season Record 11–1

PENN STATE 19 • ALABAMA 12

#31

Paterno Loss 63

STORY LINE: No. 2 Miami ends PSU's 11-game winning streak despite Heisman quarterback Gino Toretta being held to 80 passing yards. A gift touchdown from quarterback John Sacca on an interception runback and three missed field goals doom the No. 5 Lions.

SIGNIFICANCE: PSU is locked out of the major bowls by the new "Bowl Coalition," so three months before the season starts they accept an invitation to the Blockbuster Bowl. The move backfires as they have nothing to play for after the heartbreaking loss to Miami.

OCTOBER 10, 1992

UNIVERSITY PARK, PENNSYLVANIA

ATTENDANCE: 96,704

Season Record 7-5

Slogan that Fits the Story

Eye Opener for Lions

NOVEMBER 23, 2002

UNIVERSITY PARK, PENNSYLVANIA

ATTENDANCE: 108,755

#30
Paterno Win 336

STORY LINE: Running back Larry Johnson gains 279 yards in the first half and is done for the day, having become the ninth running back in NCAA history to gain 2,000 yards in a season. LJ's season average of eight yards per carry is the NCAA's best ever.

SIGNIFICANCE: The Lions move into the top 10 after suffering through two losing seasons. LJ wins the Doak Walker and Maxwell Awards and is named Walter Camp Player of the Year. Defensive linemen Jimmy Kennedy and Michael Haynes are also named All-Americans.

Season Record 9–4

PENN STATE 61 • MICHIGAN STATE 7

Paterno Win 220

STORY LINE: Quarterback Tony Sacca and running back Blair Thomas pave the way to a 41–27 lead, highlighted by wide receiver David Daniels' fabulous touchdown catch. BYU roars back behind quarterback Ty Detmer's 576 passing yards, but with the score 43–39 and the Cougars threatening, safety Gary Brown grabs the ball out of Detmer's hand as he is poised to throw and runs 53 yards for the game-clinching score.

SIGNIFICANCE: This thrilling roller-coaster ride is quite possibly the most entertaining game in PSU history.

Season Record 8–3–1

DECEMBER 29, 1989

SAN DIEGO, CALIFORNIA, HOLIDAY BOWL

ATTENDANCE: 61,113

Slogan that Fits the Story
Lions Preach to the Choir

PENN STATE 50 • BYU 39

Paws Knight Out

Mellon Bank

SEPTEMBER 24, 1988

UNIVERSITY PARK, PENNSYLVANIA

ATTENDANCE: 85,531

Slogan that Fits the Story

The Lion Sleeps ToKnight

#28
Paterno Loss 49

STORY LINE: Rutgers takes a 21–10 lead into the third quarter and holds off freshman quarterback Tony Sacca's valiant comeback effort at the 2-yard line.

SIGNIFICANCE: With five opponents ranked ahead of PSU in the preseason polls and Paterno coaching one of his most inexperienced teams ever, it is not difficult to envision the end of the Lions' amazing 49-year non-losing streak. All it would take is one upset while the rest of the favorites win. The Rutgers game is that upset.

Season Record 5–6

#27
Paterno Win 311

STORY LINE: Miami rebounds from a 17–3 deficit to take a 23–20 lead with under eight minutes to play. Things look bleak when quarterback Rashard Casey is picked off and the Canes drive to the PSU 21, but linebacker Maurice Daniels stuffs Miami on fourth-and-2 and the Lions have one last chance. Quarterback Kevin Thompson completes a stunning 79-yard touchdown pass to wide receiver Chafie Fields to pull out the win.

SIGNIFICANCE: The Lions overcome a desperate situation with one of the greatest clutch plays in PSU history.

SEPTEMBER 18, 1999

MIAMI, FLORIDA

ATTENDANCE: 74,427

Season Record 10–3

central counties bank says
This Year, Too, PSU

NOVEMBER 26, 1982

UNIVERSITY PARK, PENNSYLVANIA

ATTENDANCE: 85,522

Slogan that Fits the Story
The Pitt Patter of Defeat

#26
Paterno Win 161

STORY LINE: The Lions fall behind at halftime (7–3) as they repeatedly turn the ball over to halt promising drives. The second half is more to Paterno's liking as the defense turns in a superb goal-line stand, Nick Gancitano kicks four field goals, and quarterback Todd Blackledge tosses his record-setting 41st career touchdown pass.

SIGNIFICANCE: Penn State maintains its No. 2 ranking, thus earning its second opportunity to play for No. 1 in head-to-head competition, while thwarting No. 5 Pitt's aspirations for a national title.

Season Record 11–1

PENN STATE 19 • PITT 10

#25
Paterno Win 294

STORY LINE: PSU's early 10–0 lead dissipates as OSU's efficient passing attack creates a 27–17 deficit. But four plays later running back Aaron Harris punishes several defenders on his way to a 51-yard touchdown run. Ohio native Curtis Enis (211 yards rushing) scores on a 26-yard romp on the next drive to steal the win.

SIGNIFICANCE: The Nittany Lions give up more than 450 yards but rise to No. 1 in the polls after defeating the No. 7 Buckeyes in one of the most inspiring comeback victories of the Paterno era.

Season Record 9–3

'97

"Eye" Don't Think So

Mellon Bank

OCTOBER 11, 1997

UNIVERSITY PARK, PENNSYLVANIA

ATTENDANCE: 97,282

Slogan that Fits the Story

Wish Upon a Star, Bucks

OCTOBER 28, 1989

UNIVERSITY PARK, PENNSYLVANIA

ATTENDANCE: 85,975

#24
Paterno Loss 56

STORY LINE: Down by a point late in the fourth quarter, PSU drives 73 yards to the Alabama 6-inch line on 10 straight carries by running back Blair Thomas. With 13 seconds to play and no time-outs left, Paterno elects to kick the safe field goal, but Alabama blocks it in one of the most deflating moments in Lion history.

SIGNIFICANCE: A victory here likely would have propelled PSU to a major bowl game and a chance for a high ranking. Fans are instead left wondering if Penn State has lost its magic touch.

Season Record 8-3-1

#23

Paterno Win 123

STORY LINE: The 8–2 Panthers look primed for the upset when they carry a 10–7 lead deep into the final quarter. But a five-yard touchdown run by running back Mike Guman on a crucial fourth-down play enables PSU to preserve its No. 1 ranking.

SIGNIFICANCE: This gritty victory propels defensive tackle Bruce Clark to the Lombardi Award and quarterback Chuck Fusina to the Maxwell Award. Offensive lineman Keith Dorney, defensive tackle Matt Millen, safety Pete Harris, and kicker Matt Bahr also earn first team All-American status, the most ever in one season for the Lions.

Season Record 11–1

NOVEMBER 24, 1978

UNIVERSITY PARK, PENNSYLVANIA

ATTENDANCE: 77,465

JANUARY 1, 1992

TEMPE, ARIZONA, FIESTA BOWL

ATTENDANCE: 71,133

Slogan that Fits the Story

Tennessee Fallen-Tears

#22
Paterno Win 240

STORY LINE: The Lions grab a 7–0 lead after the Volunteers fumble the opening kickoff, but Tennessee then outgains PSU by 300 yards and takes a 17–7 lead. But midway through the third quarter, an amazing turnaround occurs, with Penn State scoring 28 points in less than four minutes by repeatedly forcing turnovers and getting easy scores, including one from linebacker Reggie Givens.

SIGNIFICANCE: As they did all season, the No. 3 Lions combine dormant periods with displays of awesome power.

Season Record 11–2

#21
Paterno Win 160

STORY LINE: Notre Dame takes a 14–13 halftime lead but is completely stymied in the second half. Quarterback Todd Blackledge and running back Curt Warner hook up for the winning touchdown on an alert audible in the fourth quarter.

SIGNIFICANCE: The Lions are ranked No. 5 going into this game as they continue to jockey for position after their loss to Alabama. This impressive win helps them move up while others falter, thereby enabling them to play in a national championship game with a win over Pitt.

Season Record 11–1

NOVEMBER 13, 1982

SOUTH BEND, INDIANA

ATTENDANCE: 59,075

114

SEPTEMBER 12, 1998

UNIVERSITY PARK, PENNSYLVANIA

ATTENDANCE: 96,291

#20
Paterno Win 300

STORY LINE: The Lions score 34 points in the first half as running back Cordell Mitchell's two long scoring runs are complemented by linebacker Lavar Arrington's interception return for six points and Bruce Branch's punt return for a touchdown.

SIGNIFICANCE: Joe Paterno celebrates his 300th victory in the same fashion as his 200th win, with a dominating win over Bowling Green made possible by the combination of a multifaceted offense and opportunistic defense and special-teams play.

Season Record 9–3

#19
Paterno Win 72

STORY LINE: On a frigid, snowy afternoon, fans watch anxiously to see who will score last in this shootout. Running back John Cappelletti's 231 yards and Gary Hayman's punt returns are enough to compensate for a shaky defense that gives up its first rushing touchdowns of the year.

SIGNIFICANCE: The Lions move to 9–0 in the signature game of a perfect season in which they dominate their other 10 opponents and hang tough in this crucial game against coach Lou Holtz.

Season Record 12–0

NOVEMBER 10, 1973

UNIVERSITY PARK, PENNSYLVANIA

ATTENDANCE: 59,424

SEPTEMBER 16, 1978

COLUMBUS, OHIO

ATTENDANCE: 88,202

Paterno Win 115

STORY LINE: An opportunistic Lion defense led by defensive tackle Bruce Clark, defensive end Larry Kubin, and safety Pete Harris shuts down the Buckeyes by forcing three fumbles and intercepting quarterback Art Schlichter five times.

SIGNIFICANCE: Matt Bahr kicks four field goals (a feat repeated three times in 1978) while Paterno gets the best of fellow coaching icon Woody Hayes in their last meeting, as Hayes is fired at year's end after punching a Clemson player at the Gator Bowl.

Season Record 11–1

PENN STATE 19 • OHIO STATE 0

117

#17
Paterno Win 194

STORY LINE: The Lions are devastating on defense, with five turnovers, five sacks, and zero red-zone plays. The offense is almost as scary, as quarterback John Shaffer completes 13 of 17 passes while his line opens up big holes for the running backs.

SIGNIFICANCE: After feasting on unranked teams for the first half of the season, the 6–0 Lions were expected to do little against the No. 2 ranked Crimson Tide. Instead, this dominating victory reveals just how powerful Penn State has become.

Season Record 12–0

OCTOBER 25, 1986

BIRMINGHAM, ALABAMA

ATTENDANCE: 60,210

SEPTEMBER 23, 2000

COLUMBUS, OHIO

ATTENDANCE: 98,144

#16
Paterno Loss 87

STORY LINE: For the fourth game in five tries, PSU scores six points or fewer. Without a ball-control offense, Paterno suffers his worst loss ever, topping the 49–11 defeat to UCLA in 1966 and the 44–6 loss to Nebraska in 1983.

SIGNIFICANCE: With just 1:39 left to play, freshman defensive back Adam Taliaferro suffers a cervical spine injury that ends his football career. Thankfully, Adam recovers and is able to lead his teammates out of the Beaver Stadium tunnel to open the 2001 season.

Season Record 5–7

PENN STATE 6 • OHIO STATE 45

#15
Paterno Win 75

STORY LINE: The Tigers open with a quick score but can do little else despite holding PSU to nine first downs. Blown calls negate two Lion touchdowns, but wide receiver Chuck Herd's sensational 72-yard fingertip touchdown catch is a highlight.

SIGNIFICANCE: Orange Bowl win number three in six years caps Paterno's third perfect season, but running back John Cappelletti's tearful Heisman Trophy dedication (to his 11-year-old brother, Joey, a victim of leukemia) provides the year's most enduring memory.

Season Record 12–0

JANUARY 1, 1974

MIAMI, FLORIDA, ORANGE BOWL

ATTENDANCE: 60,477

NOVEMBER 4, 1978

UNIVERSITY PARK,
PENNSYLVANIA

ATTENDANCE: 78,019

#14
Paterno Win 121

STORY LINE: The 8–0 Lions crush undefeated Maryland in convincing fashion, as an intimidating defense sacks and stuffs the Terps for minus-32 yards rushing while also intercepting five passes, three by safety Pete Harris.

SIGNIFICANCE: In a battle of top 5 superpowers, the Lions continue to press their claim for No. 1 by manhandling the Terrapins in yet another nightmarish outing against Paterno, who still has not lost a game to Maryland (24–0–1).

Season Record 11–1

#13
Paterno Win 264

STORY LINE: Deliriously happy fans watch in amazement as one of the most powerful college offenses ever assembled scores one quick-strike touchdown after another. Quarterback Kerry Collins (19 of 23, 265 yards) and running back Ki-Jana Carter (137 yards, four touchdowns) continue to establish their Heisman credentials. Collins goes on to win the Maxwell Award (best player) and Davey O'Brien Award (best quarterback).

SIGNIFICANCE: The Lions beat the No. 14 team in the country by 49 points in a display of true, historic greatness.

Season Record 12–0

Easy Nut to Crack

⑪ Mellon Bank

OCTOBER 29, 1994

UNIVERSITY PARK, PENNSYLVANIA

ATTENDANCE: 97,079

Slogan that Fits the Story

Bucks Pay the Price

Teddy Bearcats

Mellon Bank

OCTOBER 11, 1986

UNIVERSITY PARK, PENNSYLVANIA

ATTENDANCE: 84,812

Slogan that Fits the Story

No Escape, Claws

#12
Paterno Win 192

STORY LINE: The Lions have trouble adjusting to the Bearcats' short-passing offense and fall behind 17–14 with under six minutes to play. But the offense comes through with one of the greatest drives in PSU history. John Shaffer completes a clutch 32-yard pass to leaping running back Blair Thomas on third-and-long, and Thomas follows with four rushes for 43 yards and the winning touchdown.

SIGNIFICANCE: This fourth-quarter drive defines the character of the 1986 Lions and the course of their season.

Season Record 12–0

PENN STATE 23 • CINCINNATI 17

#11
Paterno Win 228

STORY LINE: The No. 1 Irish race out to a 21–7 halftime lead, but their star-studded offense is unable to cross midfield in the second half. Quarterback Tony Sacca (277 yards, three touchdowns) takes charge, and safety Darren Perry makes a last-minute interception to set up Craig Fayak's winning field goal as time runs out.

SIGNIFICANCE: In one of the greatest upsets in Penn State history, the No. 18 Lions execute what some regard as the finest half of football ever played during the Paterno era.

Season Record 9–3

NOVEMBER 17, 1990

SOUTH BEND, INDIANA

ATTENDANCE: 84,000

Slogan that Fits the Story
Lions Stun, Irish Stew

NOVEMBER 28, 1981

PITTSBURGH,
PENNSYLVANIA

ATTENDANCE: 60,260

#10
Paterno Win
150

STORY LINE: The Panthers quickly move out to a 14–0 lead, but Pitt quarterback Dan Marino throws an end-zone interception to cornerback Roger Jackson and the Lions pour on 48 straight points. Wide receiver Kenny Jackson makes a pirouette fake-out move on a 42-yard touchdown reception that remains legendary among Lion fans. Safety Mark Robinson picks off two passes, returning one 91 yards for a touchdown.

SIGNIFICANCE: Beating Pitt? Excellent. Embarrassing Jackie Sherrill–coached No. 1 Pitt on national TV? Priceless.

Season Record
10–2

PENN STATE 48 • PITT 14

#9
Paterno Win 269

STORY LINE: Running back Ki-Jana Carter scores on the first play (an 83-yard romp), and a resilient Nittany Lion defense holds off the pass-happy Ducks.

SIGNIFICANCE: PSU, with one of the most productive offenses in NCAA history, earns the No. 1 spot in at least eight different computer rankings with this convincing win. However, Nebraska is voted No. 1 in the traditional polls despite a weak schedule in deference to coach Tom Osborne, who trailed Paterno 2–0 in national titles entering the season.

JANUARY 2, 1995

PASADENA, CALIFORNIA, ROSE BOWL

ATTENDANCE: 102,247

Season Record 12–0

#8
Paterno Loss 44

STORY LINE: After a promising start in which the 11–0 Lions score a touchdown on their first drive, turnovers limit the offense to one field goal while the more efficient Sooners methodically rack up 25 points.

SIGNIFICANCE: PSU loses a national title game for the second time, but this loss is not nearly as painful as the 1978 Sugar Bowl defeat, as few expected the offensively limited Nittany Lions to run the table in 1985. Plus, Paterno will get another shot at No. 1 soon.

JANUARY 1, 1986

MIAMI, FLORIDA,
ORANGE BOWL

ATTENDANCE: 74,148

Season Record 11–1

#7
Paterno Loss
81

STORY LINE: A seesaw game comes down to a desperation drive. With the 9–0 Lions leading 23–21, the defense forces a fourth-and-18 last-ditch pass. But Gophers wide receiver Arland Bruce makes a miraculous shoestring catch off a deflected ball, setting up the winning field goal and dashing PSU's championship aspirations.

SIGNIFICANCE: Only a traumatic shock could disrupt the 1999 team's pursuit of another national title for coach Paterno. Some believe that the Lions still have not recovered from this devastating loss.

Season Record
10–3

'99

Easy Come, Easy Gopher

Ⓜ **Mellon Bank**

NOVEMBER 6, 1999

UNIVERSITY PARK, PENNSYLVANIA

ATTENDANCE: 96,753

Slogan that Fits the Story

Gophers Dig Deep

PSU —
Nois Control

Mellon Bank

NOVEMBER 12, 1994

CHAMPAIGN, ILLINOIS

ATTENDANCE: 72,364

Slogan that Fits the Story

No More
Sparkle in
Champaign

#6
Paterno Win 266

STORY LINE: The Illini stun the Lions with three first-quarter touchdowns, but PSU moves 99 yards to close the gap to 21–7. With six minutes to go, Penn State—still down 31–28—forces a punt, but it is downed on the 4-yard line, 96 yards from pay dirt. In what will forever be known as "The Drive," quarterback Kerry Collins and crew save the season with a perfectly executed mix of runs and passes.

SIGNIFICANCE: This is the game that transforms the 1994 season from mere greatness to mythical status.

Season Record 12–0

#5
Paterno Win 324

'01
Nuttin' Doin', Buckeyes

Mellon Bank

STORY LINE: Quarterback Zack Mills leads a heroic comeback after OSU takes a 27–9 lead. The rally starts with a 69-yard touchdown run in which Mills leaps over and bounces off several defenders and ends with two touchdown passes. The Bucks' last-ditch field-goal try late in the fourth quarter is blocked by cornerback Bryan Scott.

SIGNIFICANCE: Coach Paterno passes old nemesis Bear Bryant with win number 324 and becomes college football's career victory leader in one of the greatest games of his coaching career.

OCTOBER 27, 2001

UNIVERSITY PARK, PENNSYLVANIA

ATTENDANCE: 108,327

Season Record 5–6

Slogan that Fits the Story

Nutcracker Sweet

SEPTEMBER 25, 1982

UNIVERSITY PARK,
PENNSYLVANIA

ATTENDANCE: 85,304

#4
Paterno Win 155

STORY LINE: The Lions build a 21–7 advantage despite missing three field goals, but the Huskers fight back and take a 24–21 lead with 1:18 left to play. Quarterback Todd Blackledge converts on fourth-and-11 and then completes a controversial pass to tight end Mike McCloskey (in bounds at the 2?). With nine seconds remaining, a disputed shoestring touchdown catch by tight end Kirk "Stonehands" Bowman clinches the win.

SIGNIFICANCE: Many regard this thrilling comeback victory as the most exciting game in Beaver Stadium history.

Season Record 11–1

PENN STATE 27 • NEBRASKA 24

#3

Paterno Loss
25

STORY LINE: Penn State struggles throughout the game, throwing four interceptions and rushing for only 19 yards. Crucial penalties and a blown call on Alabama's first touchdown (actually an incomplete pass) also hurt. Still, the most memorable plays are the unsuccessful third- and fourth-down dives by running backs Matt Suhey and Mike Guman from inside the 1 midway through the fourth quarter.

SIGNIFICANCE: Paterno agonizes over being outcoached by Bear Bryant and losing his first national title game.

JANUARY 1, 1979

NEW ORLEANS, LOUISIANA,
SUGAR BOWL

ATTENDANCE: 76,824

Season Record
11–1

LIONS #1 NO BULL! SUGAR BOWL '83
central counties bank says
cb

JANUARY 1, 1983

NEW ORLEANS, LOUISIANA,
SUGAR BOWL

ATTENDANCE: 78,124

Slogan that Fits the Story
Blue Knocked the Dogs Out

#2
Paterno Win 162

STORY LINE: Running back Curt Warner again outshines a Heisman winner (running back Herschel Walker), but it is wide receiver Greg Garrity whose diving fourth-quarter, 47-yard touchdown catch provides the winning score and the game's most memorable moment.

SIGNIFICANCE: No. I at last! Penn State becomes the first team to win a national championship with more passing than rushing yards and with a schedule rated as the toughest in the NCAA. Todd Blackledge takes home the Davey O'Brien Award as the nation's top quarterback.

Season Record 11–1

PENN STATE 27 • GEORGIA 23

#1
Paterno Win 199

STORY LINE: The big-talking Canes arrive in combat fatigues, but the real heroes are linebacker Shane Conlan, punter John Bruno, and a secondary that intimidates Miami's receivers with devastating hits. The game ends with linebacker Pete Giftopoulos' joyful goal-line interception, number five for Miami quarterback Vinny Testaverde.

SIGNIFICANCE: Penn State celebrates its 100th year of football by winning its second national championship in an epic battle often regarded as one of the greatest college games ever played.

Season Record 12–0

JANUARY 2, 1987

TEMPE, ARIZONA, FIESTA BOWL

ATTENDANCE: 73,098

 Sunkist Fiesta Bowl 1987 #1 NITTANY 1 LIONS Blow Out the Hurricanes — Mellon Bank

 Slogan that Fits the Story — Hurricanes Are Blowhards

PENN STATE 14 • MIAMI 10

APPENDIX

THE COMPLETE COLLECTION OF
PENN STATE
FOOTBALL BUTTONS
1972–2003

In the previous pages, we described our born-and-bred enthusiasm for Penn State and our appreciation of the role that Joe Paterno has played in the growth and progress of the football program and the university. You also read about coach Paterno's cycles of excellence that reliably return the Penn State football team to King of Beasts status every several years. In addition, we presented our expert and colorful (but undoubtedly controversial) ranking of the 100 most significant games in the Paterno era, including giving you the actual football button image and slogan for each of those memorable games as well as an alternative slogan that might have been selected had the game's outcome been known in advance. Now we proudly present our self-designated official and complete collection of the Penn State football buttons.

For 32 years, the Penn State football buttons have symbolized the pride and spirit of Nittany Lions fans worldwide for a great university, a football program of national stature, and its legendary coach, Joe Paterno. Through three bank sponsors, hundreds of players, and thousands of fans, these buttons represent one of the longest continuous promotions of a college sports program in the nation. Not surprisingly, the buttons have also become a collectible for many people. We suspect that looking at the following pages will cause many of you, even those who have not been bitten by the button-collecting bug, to search long-forgotten boxes in the attic and basement to recover buttons you once picked up on game day. If you find one, enjoy the moment, and then return to this book to learn more about it.

The authors admit that they are serious collectors of these buttons and serious button slogan

Burn Wake Forest	1974		Spartan is Sweet Sorrow	1998
Wrong Anther Panther	1983		Errorzona	1999
It's Feudal: Knights	1984		Pitt To Be Tied	1999
No Santa Here, Virginia	1989		Easy Come, Easy Gopher	1999
Give Rutgers Knightmares	1990		No Green Giant Here	1999
MD—You'll Need One	1991		No Free Launch Here	2000
A B-C D-Feat	1992		MSU – Green With Envy	2000
All Hawk and No Action	1993		Lions Won't Need a Recount	2001
Knightly News: Lions Win	1994		Iowa's On The Hawk Seat	2001
Sleepless in Ann Arbor	1994		Nuttin' Doin', Buckeyes	2001
Easy Nut to Crack	1994		It Isn't Easy Being Green	2001
That's Owl She Wrote	1995		Get Reel, Virginia	2001
It's Pay Buck Time	1996		Lions Make Blue Cheese	2002
Hoosier Worst Knightmare? PSU	1996		You ARE The Weakest Cat	2002
Lions – King Among Cats	1996		Champaign, You're Toast	2002
Not a Pitty Picture	1997		Wahoos Sorry Now	2002
Driving Mich Crazy	1997		Kick Wisconsin's Dairy Air	2003
Lions Let Off Steam	1997		Lions Put The Cat Out	2003
You're In Deep, Purple	1998		Braggers Can't Be Hoosiers	2003
No Oscar for Madison	1998			

writers. In fact, on the previous page, 39 slogans (10 percent of all the button slogans written to date) have come from members of our family.

Our ability to present ourselves as the definitive experts on these buttons is the result of help from many others, including Mimi Fredman (the originator of the button promotion and writer of this book's preface), Penn State University representatives, representatives from the bank sponsors, and last but certainly not least, our fellow button collectors. We think we have identified every Penn State football bank button ever made, all of which are presented season by season on the pages that follow. We even include a "special" button page honoring specific achievements and a "variations" page that identifies unique alternative versions of several of these buttons. We represent this as the "Complete Collection," although it would not surprise us if someone were to come up with one that we missed. That is a great part of the fun of collecting, and we look forward to hearing from all who would challenge our self-proclaimed expertise on this topic.

To help you become an expert too, here are 15 "button trivia" facts that if strategically used at your next football tailgate will allow you to amaze family, friends, and fellow Penn State fans with your button knowledge.

1. Buttons have been produced for all games since 1972, except for 1972 away games.

2. Central Counties Bank sponsored the buttons from 1972 until 1983. After acquiring Central Counties Bank, Mellon Bank continued as the sponsor from 1984 until the middle of 2001, and since then Citizens Bank has been the sponsor.

3. All buttons include the sponsoring bank's logo with two exceptions: home games in 1972 (actually, except for the first two home games in 1972, there are even "versions" of the buttons for that year with the bank logo), and Pitt games from 1986 through 1991 (presumably because Mellon Bank is headquartered in Pittsburgh).

4. Prior to the beginning of the 2001 season, all of the game buttons for that year were produced with Mellon Bank's logo on them. However, as a result of Citizens Bank's midyear takeover of the button program, an additional run of buttons was produced for the last three home games with Citizens' logo on them, thus resulting in those games having two different versions of the same button—one with Mellon's logo and one with Citizens' logo.

5. During some seasons in the past and currently, button slogans (except for bowl games) have been selected from public submissions in a contest run by the sponsoring bank. Not surprisingly, Joe Paterno has historically had a say in approving slogans.

6. Only two slogans have been repeated. The 1972 and 1975 Iowa games both had the slogan "Hammer the Hawkeyes," which you can tell apart because the 1972 button was made with a green cardboard pin back and the 1975 button had a metal pin back. In addition, the 1975 and 1982 Syracuse games both used the slogan "Abuse Syracuse." These are harder to tell apart, but the key is that the 1975 slogan used larger type than the 1982 slogan.

7. Referencing Penn State's mascot is a good way to maximize your chances in the slogan contest, because 39 slogans have included the word *Lion, Lions,* or *Lion's.*

8. The first "run" of buttons for the 1972 season was made with green cardboard pin backs because it was a cheaper button type that kept the cost lower for the sponsoring bank when it was not yet known how popular these buttons would become. Later that season, with demand for the buttons soaring, additional buttons were made incorporating the Central Counties

Bank logo. Finally that year, versions of the North Carolina State and Pitt game buttons were made using metal pin backs. The metal pin back has been the standard ever since.

9. All buttons are 2¼ inches in diameter except for the buttons manufactured in 1972 and 1973 (when they were 2 inches in diameter) and two 1978 "Special" nongame buttons (one oversized and one oval-shaped).

10. There are three categories of buttons. *Regular Season* buttons have a blue background and white letters (there are two exceptions in 1993 in which the colors are reversed to commemorate historically significant games). *Bowl Game* buttons have a white background and blue letters (there are three exceptions in which the colors are reversed: the 1974 Orange Bowl, the 1975 Cotton Bowl [which was made both ways], and the 1986 Orange Bowl). Finally, five *"Special"* nongame buttons have been produced, each with a white background and blue letters.

11. *Regular Season* buttons were dated with the year in 1983, 1984, and from 1997 to the present, as well as for the first Big Ten game with Minnesota in

1993 and Penn State's 1,000[th] football game, with Michigan, in 1993. *Bowl Game* buttons have been dated since 1982, as was the button for the 1979 Sugar Bowl against Alabama. Three of the five *"Special"* nongame buttons also are dated.

12. One season's buttons, 1984, include a white background stripe across the middle of the button.

13. Only three buttons have a color on them other than blue and white: the 1986 Orange Bowl (orange), the 1987 Fiesta Bowl (yellow, red, and orange), and the 1995 Rose Bowl (red).

14. Five buttons have a Nittany Lion image on them.

15. Consistent with the sponsoring banks' intention that the buttons be given away free to promote community spirit and pride in the Lions, the buttons have also become a means of charitable fundraising. Specifically, the Nittany Lion Club has used the buttons to help raise money for the Norm Constantine Fund. Norm Constantine was a former Nittany Lion who was tragically paralyzed in an automobile accident. This fund, which first helped Norm's family pay for his medical expenses, later, after his death, served to provide a scholarship for the student who performs as the Nittany Lion mascot. Recently, these funds were determined to be fully endowed. It has been suggested that in the future money raised from the buttons be directed to a new fund, established in 2003, called the "Back the Lions Raise the Roar Endowment." This fund has been established to aid in the development and growth of the Penn State Blue Band, cheerleaders, and dance team. In keeping with the longstanding charitable role the buttons have played, a portion of the proceeds from the sale of this book will go to the "Back the Lions Raise the Roar Endowment."

Whether you are a serious collector, or inspired by this book to start a collection, or just want to know which game goes with the button you found in the back of your dresser drawer, the following pages will serve as your "official" guide to the Penn State football buttons. If you are a student, an alum, a fan, or just one of the numerous people with Penn State connections, don't be surprised if you start reliving your past association with Penn State, because for us—and we suspect for you—these buttons often evoke memories of far more than football. Enjoy your trip down memory lane, and FIGHT ON, STATE!

Penn State 21
Navy 10

Penn State 37
N.C. State 22

Penn State 14
Iowa 10

Penn State 49
Pitt 27

Penn State 17
Syracuse 0

Penn State 46
Maryland 16

Oklahoma 14
Penn State 0
(Sugar Bowl)

143

Penn State 20
at Stanford 6

Penn State 54
Army 3

Penn State 35
N.C. State 29

Gore the Goat
Penn State 39
at Navy 0

Penn State 49
at Syracuse 6

Penn State 49
Ohio U. 10

Halt the Hawkeyes
Penn State 27
Iowa 8

Mash the Mounties
Penn State 62
West Virginia 14

Penn State 35
Pitt 13

Penn State 19
at Air Force 9

Tear the Terrapins
Penn State 42
at Maryland 22

Penn State 16
LSU 9
(Orange Bowl)

144

Penn State 24
Stanford 20

Penn State 55
Wake Forest 0

at N.C. State 12
Penn State 7

Navy 7
Penn State 6

Penn State 30
Syracuse 14

Penn State 35
Ohio U. 16

Penn State 27
at Iowa 0

Penn State 21
at West Virginia 12

Penn State 31
at Pitt 10
(Three Rivers
Stadium)

Penn State 21
at Army 14

Penn State 24
Maryland 17

Penn State 41
Baylor 20
(Cotton Bowl)

145

Penn State 26
at Temple 25
(Franklin Field)

Penn State 15
at Maryland 13

Penn State 10
Kentucky 3

Penn State 34
Stanford 14

Penn State 39
West Virginia 0

N.C. State 15
Penn State 14

at Ohio State 17
Penn State 9

Penn State 19
at Syracuse 7

Penn State 7
at Pitt 6
(Three Rivers
Stadium)

Penn State 30
at Iowa 10

Alabama 13
Penn State 6
(Sugar Bowl)

Penn State 31
Army 0

Stifle Stanford

Penn State 15
Stanford 12

Goodnite, Knights

Penn State 41
N.C. State 20

Scatter the Pack

Penn State 38
Army 16

Batter the Bucks

Ohio State 12
Penn State 7

Squeeze the Orange

Penn State 21
at Miami 7

Storm Over Miami

Penn State 27
Syracuse 3

Hammer the Hawkeyes

Iowa 7
Penn State 6

Stew WVU

at Pitt 24
Penn State 7
(Three Rivers
Stadium)

Prune Pitt

Penn State 33
at West Virginia 0

Cool the Cats

at Kentucky 22
Penn State 6

Trample Temple

Notre Dame 20
Penn State 9
(Gator Bowl)

Stew the Irish

Penn State 31
at Temple 30
(Veterans Stadium)

Table
the
Knights

Penn State 45
at Rutgers 7
(Giants
Stadium)

Paw
Utah

Penn State 16
Utah State 7

Penn State 21
at N.C. State 17

Cry,
Wolf

Space
Out
Houston

Penn State 31
Houston 14

Grind
the Rind

Penn State 31
at Syracuse 24

Penn State 44
Temple 7

Hoot on
Temple

Bloody
Mary-
Land

Penn State 27
Maryland 9

Smear
Mountain-
eers

Penn State 49
West Virginia 28

Penn State 15
at Pitt 13

Make
Pitt Stop

Fry
Kentucky

Kentucky 24
Penn State 20

SLAM
MI-AM

Penn State 49
Miami 7

Penn State 42
Arizona State 30
(Fiesta Bowl)

LEVEL
THE
DEVILS

148

 Penn State 10
at Temple 7
(Veterans
Stadium)

 Penn State 58
TCU 0

Penn State 27
Maryland 3

 Penn State 26
Rutgers 10

 Penn State 30
at Kentucky 0

Penn State 19
N.C. State 10

 Penn State 19
at Ohio State 0

Penn State 45
Syracuse 15

Penn State 17
Pitt 10

 Penn State 49
at West Virginia 21

Penn State 26
SMU 21

 Alabama 14
Penn State 7
(Sugar Bowl)

149

Fix the Ruts

Penn State 45
Rutgers 10

Discharge Army

Penn State 24
Army 3

Penn State 9
at N.C. State 7

Shuffle the Pack

Bag the Aggies

Texas A&M 27
Penn State 14

Can the Juice

Penn State 35
Syracuse 7
(Giants Stadium)

Penn State 22
Temple 7

Prey on Temple

Husk the Huskers

at Nebraska 42
Penn State 17

Chew WVU

Penn State 31
West Virginia 6

Pitt 29
Penn State 14

Pity Pitt

Turtle Soup

Penn State 27
at Maryland 7

Shoot the Breeze

Miami 26
Penn State 10

Penn State 9
Tulane 6
(Liberty Bowl)

Wave Good-bye

Penn State 54
Colgate 10

Penn State 21
N.C. State 13

Penn State 24
at Maryland 10

Penn State 25
at Texas A&M 9

Penn State 50
at Temple 7
(Veterans Stadium)

Penn State 24
Syracuse 7

Nebraska 21
Penn State 7

Penn State 20
at West Virginia 15

Pitt 14
Penn State 9

Penn State 29
at Missouri 21

Penn State 27
Miami 12

Penn State 31
Ohio State 19
(Fiesta Bowl)

Penn State 52
Cincinnati 0

Penn State 41
at Syracuse 16

Alabama 31
Penn State 16

Penn State 30
at Nebraska 24

Penn State 30
West Virginia 7

Penn State 24
Notre Dame 21

Penn State 30
Temple 0

Penn State 48
at Pitt 14
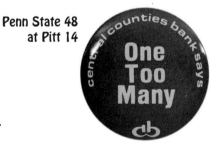

at Miami 17
Penn State 14

Penn State 38
Boston College 7

Penn State 22
at N.C. State 15

Penn State 26
USC 10
(Fiesta Bowl)

152

 Penn State 31
Temple 14

 Penn State 54
N.C. State 0

at Alabama 42
Penn State 21
(Legion Field)

 Penn State 39
Maryland 31

Penn State 24
at Notre Dame 14

Penn State 28
Syracuse 7

 Penn State 49
Rutgers 14

Penn State 19
Pitt 10

Penn State 24
at West Virginia 0

 Penn State 27
Nebraska 24

Penn State 27
Georgia 23
(Sugar Bowl)

Penn State 52
at Boston College 17

153

Nebraska 44
Penn State 6
(Giants Stadium)

Surely You Joust

Penn State 36
at Rutgers 25
(Giants Stadium)

at Boston College 27
Penn State 17
(Sullivan Stadium)

Tough Beans, B.C.

Cincinnati 14
Penn State 3

W.H.I.P. Cincinnati

'Terno The Tide

Penn State 34
Alabama 28

Penn State 38
Brown 21

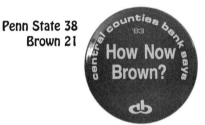

How Now Brown?

Iowa 42
Penn State 34

Hawkeyes Eat Quiche

Knock 'Em Seedless

Penn State 17
at Syracuse 6

Penn State 34
Notre Dame 30

Italian Eyes Smiling

Penn State 23
at Temple 18
(Veterans
Stadium)

Owl Be Darned

Welcome To Everest

Penn State 41
West Virginia 23

Penn State 24
at Pitt 24

Wrong Anther Panther

Sit!

'83
Aloha Bowl

Penn State 13
Washington 10
(Aloha Bowl)

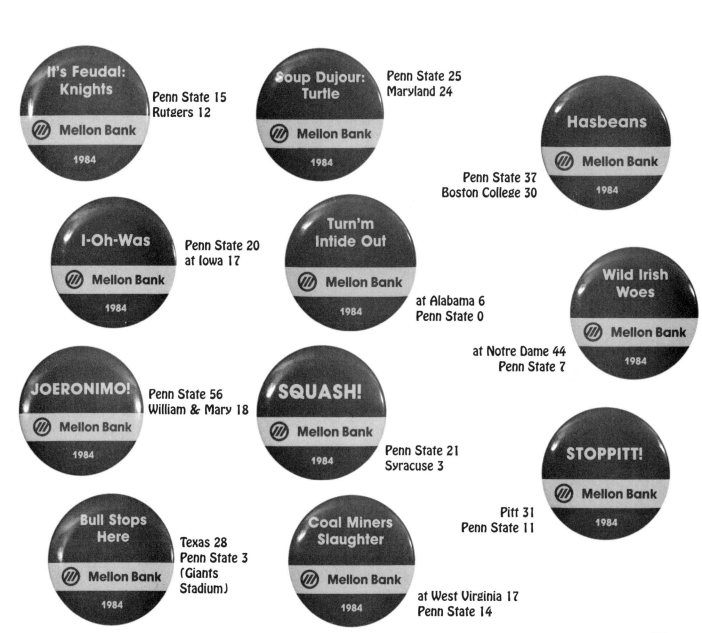

It's Feudal: Knights
Mellon Bank
1984

Penn State 15
Rutgers 12

Soup Dujour: Turtle
Mellon Bank
1984

Penn State 25
Maryland 24

Hasbeans
Mellon Bank
1984

Penn State 37
Boston College 30

I-Oh-Was
Mellon Bank
1984

Penn State 20
at Iowa 17

Turn'm Intide Out
Mellon Bank
1984

at Alabama 6
Penn State 0

Wild Irish Woes
Mellon Bank
1984

at Notre Dame 44
Penn State 7

JOERONIMO!
Mellon Bank
1984

Penn State 56
William & Mary 18

SQUASH!
Mellon Bank
1984

Penn State 21
Syracuse 3

STOPPITT!
Mellon Bank
1984

Pitt 31
Penn State 11

Bull Stops Here
Mellon Bank
1984

Texas 28
Penn State 3
(Giants Stadium)

Coal Miners Slaughter
Mellon Bank
1984

at West Virginia 17
Penn State 14

155

Penn State 20
at Maryland 18

Penn State 19
Alabama 17

Penn State 31
at Cincinnati 10
(Riverfront
Stadium)

Penn State 27
Temple 25

Penn State 24
at Syracuse 20

Penn State 36
Notre Dame 6

Penn State 17
East Carolina 10

Penn State 27
West Virginia 0

Penn State 31
at Pitt 0

Penn State 17
at Rutgers 10
(Giants
Stadium)

Penn State 16
Boston College 12

Oklahoma 25
Penn State 10
(Orange Bowl)

Penn State 45
Temple 15

Teddy Bearcats

Penn State 17
Maryland 15

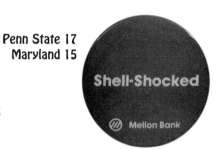
Shell-Shocked

Penn State 23
Cincinnati 17

Penn State 26
at Boston
College 14
(Sullivan
Stadium)

Fruitless Effort

Penn State 24
at Notre Dame 19

Begorra & Begone

Penn State 42
Syracuse 3

Penn State 42
East Carolina 17

Up Tide Down

Penn State 34
Pitt 14

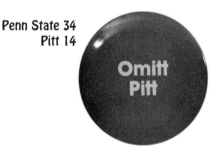
Omitt Pitt

Penn State 23
at Alabama 3

Penn State 31
Rutgers 6

Pierced "Eers"

Penn State 14
Miami 10
(Fiesta Bowl)

Penn State 19
at West Virginia 0

157

Lions Bowling Party

Ⓜ Mellon Bank

Penn State 45
Bowling Green 19

PSU — Temple of Doom

Ⓜ Mellon Bank

Penn State 27
Temple 13

Penn State 21
at Maryland 16
(Memorial Stadium)

Soup's On

Ⓜ Mellon Bank

Joe Pa's In, Tide's Out

Ⓜ Mellon Bank

Alabama 24
Penn State 13

Good Knight Scarlet

Ⓜ Mellon Bank

Penn State 35
Rutgers 21

at Pitt 10
Penn State 0

PSU — Top Cat

Cat-Tastrophe

Ⓜ Mellon Bank

Penn State 41
Cincinnati 0

Bruise Syracuse

Ⓜ Mellon Bank

at Syracuse 48
Penn State 21

Penn State 21
Notre Dame 20

Irish Eyes Are Crying

Ⓜ Mellon Bank

No "Cheers" Here

Ⓜ Mellon Bank

Penn State 27
at Boston College 17
(Sullivan Stadium)

Just a Miner Detail

Ⓜ Mellon Bank

Penn State 25
West Virginia 21

Clemson 35
Penn State 10
(Citrus Bowl)

FLORIDA CITRUS BOWL • JANUARY 1, 1988
Lions' Pride Takes Clemson's Hide

Ⓜ Mellon Bank

Boo Hoo Wa-Hoos!

Mellon Bank

Penn State 42
at Virginia 14

PSU Over WKRP!

Mellon Bank

Penn State 35
Cincinnati 9

Penn State 17
Maryland 10

Lions Shell It Out!

Mellon Bank

Sore Like An Eagle

Mellon Bank

Penn State 23
Boston College 20

Are You Syrious?

Mellon Bank

Pitt 14
Penn State 7

Another Pittfall

Syracuse 24
Penn State 10

Paws Knight Out

Mellon Bank

Rutgers 21
Penn State 16

Wipe Out

Mellon Bank

at Notre Dame 21
Penn State 3

N D — No Danger

Mellon Bank

at Alabama 8
Penn State 3
(Legion Field)

Owl, In a Days Work

Mellon Bank

Penn State 45
at Temple 9
(Veterans Stadium)

Take 'em Home

Mellon Bank

at West Virginia 51
Penn State 30

159

No Santa Here, Virginia

@ Mellon Bank

Virginia 14
Penn State 6

Sorely, You Joust

@ Mellon Bank

Penn State 13
at Maryland 13
(Memorial Stadium)

Penn State 17
at Rutgers 0
(Giants Stadium)

Rigor Tortoise

@ Mellon Bank

Owl Washed Up

@ Mellon Bank

Penn State 42
Temple 3

Carrier Pigeons

@ Mellon Bank

Penn State 34
at Syracuse 12

Notre Dame 34
Penn State 23

Notre Tamed

@ Mellon Bank

BC — Ancient History

@ Mellon Bank

Penn State 7
Boston College 3

Crimson Cried

@ Mellon Bank

Penn State 16
at Pitt 13

Have No Pitt-y

Alabama 17
Penn State 16

Wronghorns

@ Mellon Bank

Penn State 16
at Texas 12

Mountains Into Mole Hills

@ Mellon Bank

Penn State 19
West Virginia 9

Penn State 50
BYU 39
(Holiday Bowl)

SEA WORLD HOLIDAY BOWL • DECEMBER 29, 1989
BLUE BY U

@ Mellon Bank

Texas 17
Penn State 13

Penn State 27
Syracuse 21

Penn State 24
Maryland 10

at USC 19
Penn State 14

Penn State 24
at Notre Dame 21

Penn State 40
at Boston College 21

Penn State 28
Rutgers 0

Penn State 22
Pitt 17

Penn State 9
at Alabama 0

Penn State 48
Temple 10

Florida State 24
Penn State 17
(Blockbuster Bowl)

Penn State 31
at West Virginia 19

161

 **Buzz Off!**

Penn State 34
Georgia Tech 22
(Giants Stadium)

 **Lions' Tea Party**

Penn State 51
West Virginia 6

 **Up to Their 'Eers in Lions**

Penn State 28
Boston College 21

 **They're Barely Cats!**

Penn State 81
Cincinnati 0

Feather Duster

Penn State 47
at Maryland 7
(Memorial Stadium)

 **MD— You'll Need One**

Penn State 24
at Temple 7
(Veterans Stadium)

USC— Back to the Beach!

at USC 21
Penn State 10

 **Storm's Over**

Penn State 35
Notre Dame 13

Lion Eyes are Smilin'

at Miami 26
Penn State 20

Brigham To Their Knees

Penn State 33
BYU 7

Penn State 32
at Pitt 20

 It's Joust About Over

 Tempe, Arizona • January 1, 1992 **PSU — the Besta Fiesta**

A Lion Pittnic

Penn State 37
Rutgers 17

Penn State 42
Tennessee 17
(Fiesta Bowl)

162

Penn State 24
at Cincinnati 20

Penn State 38
at Rutgers 24
(Giants Stadium)

at BYU 30
Penn State 17

Penn State 49
Temple 8

Miami 17
Penn State 14

at Notre Dame 17
Penn State 16

Penn State 52
Eastern Michigan 7

Boston College 35
Penn State 32

Penn State 57
Pitt 13

Penn State 49
Maryland 13

Penn State 40
at West Virginia 26

Stanford 24
Penn State 3
(Blockbuster Bowl)

163

Penn State 38
Minnesota 20

Penn State 70
at Maryland 7

Penn State 28
Illinois 14

Penn State 21
USC 20

Penn State 43
at Northwestern 21

Michigan 21
Penn State 13

Penn State 31
at Iowa 0

Penn State 38
at Michigan State 37

at Ohio State 24
Penn State 6

Penn State 31
Rutgers 7

Penn State 38
Indiana 31

Penn State 31
Tennessee 13
(Citrus Bowl)

 Goph Busters
Mellon Bank

Penn State 56
at Minnesota 3

 A Moot Hoot
Mellon Bank

Penn State 35
at Illinois 31

 PSU — Nois Control
Mellon Bank

Penn State 48
at Temple 21
(Franklin Field)

Troy Troy Again
Mellon Bank

Penn State 38
USC 14

 Sleepless in Ann Arbor
Mellon Bank

Penn State 45
Northwestern 17

 Wildcan'ts
Mellon Bank

Penn State 31
at Michigan 24

Eye Don't Think So
Mellon Bank

Penn State 61
Iowa 21

 Easy Nut to Crack
Mellon Bank

Penn State 59
Michigan State 31

 Deja Vu... MSU
Mellon Bank

Penn State 63
Ohio State 14

Knightly News: Lions Win
Mellon Bank

Penn State 55
Rutgers 27

 Knock Knock — Hoosier?
Mellon Bank

Penn State 38
Oregon 20
(Rose Bowl)

 PASADENA, CALIFORNIA
Can't Duck the Lions
Mellon Bank
JANUARY 2, 1995

Penn State 35
at Indiana 29

165

 Penn State 24
Texas Tech 23

The Buckeyes Stop Here

at Northwestern 21
Penn State 10

Lions Are
The Top Cats

Ohio State 28
Penn State 25

 Penn State 66
Temple 14

Subdue Purdue

Penn State 27
Michigan 17

Michigan Impossible

Penn State 26
at Purdue 23

This Knight's Ours

Penn State 59
at Rutgers 34
(Giants Stadium)

I-owa Doubt It

Penn State 24
at Michigan State 20

Big MichStake

Penn State 41
at Iowa 27

Lions Will Not Be Badgered

Wisconsin 17
Penn State 9

Hoo's Sorry Now

Penn State 43
Auburn 14
(Outback Bowl)

OUTBACK BOWL, JANUARY 1, 1996
PSU-Topcats of the Outback
Mellon Bank
TAMPA, FLORIDA

Penn State 45
Indiana 21

166

Penn State 24
USC 7
(Giants Stadium)

Too Badger Facing Lions

Penn State 23
at Wisconsin 20

Penn State 48
at Indiana 26

Hoosier Worst Nightmare? PSU

Shuffle the Cards

Penn State 24
Louisville 7

It's Pay Buck Time

at Ohio State 38
Penn State 7

Penn State 34
Northwestern 9

Lions — King Among Cats

Lions Don't Pull Sleds

Penn State 49
Northern Illinois 0

Burst Their Pipe Dreams

Penn State 31
Purdue 14

Penn State 29
at Michigan 17

No Safe Harbor in Ann Arbor

Penn State 41
Temple 0
(Giants Stadium)

I'll be Hooting for the Lions

Ground the Hawks

Iowa 21
Penn State 20

Penn State 32
Michigan State 29

Disheartened Spartan

FIESTA BOWL, JANUARY 1, 1997
PSU Fiesta- Texas Siesta
Mellon Bank
TEMPE, ARIZONA

Penn State 38
Texas 15
(Fiesta Bowl)

167

1997

Season Record:
Won 9, Lost 3;
in Big Ten: 6–2, 2nd

Final Rankings:
AP 16th,
USA Today/ESPN 17th

Penn State 34
Pitt 17

Penn State 42
at Purdue 17

Penn State 52
Temple 10

Penn State 35
Wisconsin 10

Penn State 16
Minnesota 15

Penn State 41
at Illinois 6

at Michigan State 49
Penn State 14

Penn State 30
at Northwestern 27

Florida 21
Penn State 6
(Citrus Bowl)

Penn State 31
Ohio State 27

Penn State 57
at Louisville 21

Michigan 34
Penn State 8

Penn State 34
Southern
Mississippi 6

Penn State 41
Northwestern 10

Penn State 27
at Minnesota 17

Penn State 48
Bowling Green 3

at Wisconsin 24
Penn State 3

Penn State 31
Purdue 13

Penn State 20
at Pitt 13

Penn State 51
Michigan State 28

Penn State 27
Illinois 0

at Ohio State 28
Penn State 9

Penn State 26
Kentucky 14
(Outback Bowl)

at Michigan State 27
Penn State 0

169

 Errorzona

Penn State 41
Arizona 7

 Indi-Sposed

Penn State 27
at Illinois 7

 Illinoyance

Penn State 45
Indiana 24

 Tire Out Akron

Penn State 70
Akron 24

 Feather's In Joe's Cap

Minnesota 24
Penn State 23

 Easy Come, Easy Gopher

Penn State 31
at Iowa 7

 Pitt To Be Tied

Penn State 20
Pitt 17

 Don't It Make Your Buckeyes Blue

Michigan 31
Penn State 27

Penn State 23
Ohio State 10

 You Wish, Mich

Penn State 27
at Miami 23

PSU-Storm Troopers

 Much Purdue About Nothing

at Michigan State 35
Penn State 28

 Remember the LIONS!

No Green Giant Here

Penn State 31
at Purdue 25

Penn State 24
Texas A&M 0
(Alamo Bowl)

170

'00
Southern Cal Can't
Ⓜ Mellon Bank

USC 29
Penn State 5
(Giants Stadium)

'00
Outta Luck-Eyes
Ⓜ Mellon Bank

at Ohio State 45
Penn State 6

Penn State 27
at Indiana 24
(RCA Dome)

'00
Indi-gestion
Ⓜ Mellon Bank

'00
No Free Launch Here
Ⓜ Mellon Bank

Toledo 24
Penn State 6

'00
Take the Steam Out
Ⓜ Mellon Bank

Penn State 22
Purdue 20

Iowa 26
Penn State 23

'00
Fowled Out
Ⓜ Mellon Bank

'00
All Bark and No Bite
Ⓜ Mellon Bank

Penn State 67
Louisiana Tech 7

'00
www. go-pher-it .psu
Ⓜ Mellon Bank

at Minnesota 25
Penn State 16

at Michigan 33
Penn State 11

'00
Ann Arbor, Who's She?
Ⓜ Mellon Bank

'00
Lions Gitt itt Done
Ⓜ Mellon Bank

at Pitt 12
Penn State 0

'00
ill-advised
Ⓜ Mellon Bank

Penn State 39
Illinois 25

Penn State 42
Michigan State 23

'00
MSU- Green With Envy
Ⓜ Mellon Bank

171

Miami 33
Penn State 7

Penn State 38
at Northwestern 35

Penn State 28
Indiana 14

Wisconsin 18
Penn State 6

Penn State 29
Ohio State 27

Penn State 42
at Michigan State 37

at Iowa 24
Penn State 18

Penn State 38
Southern Mississippi 20

at Virginia 20
Penn State 14

Michigan 20
Penn State 0

at Illinois 33
Penn State 28

172

Knightmare · CITIZENS BANK

Penn State 27
Central Florida 24

Lions Make Blue Cheese · CITIZENS BANK

Penn State 34
at Wisconsin 31

Penn State 18
Illinois 7

Champaign, You're Toast · CITIZENS BANK

Settlin The Score For '94 · CITIZENS BANK

Penn State 40
Nebraska 7

Lions, Bring Down The Big House · CITIZENS BANK

at Michigan 27
Penn State 24
(OT)

Penn State 35
Virginia 14

Wahoos Sorry Now · CITIZENS BANK

It's A Cat Eat Dog World · CITIZENS BANK

Penn State 49
Louisiana Tech 17

You ARE The Weakest Cat · CITIZENS BANK

Penn State 49
Northwestern 0

Penn State 58
at Indiana 25

Joe's Our Man... Hoosiers? · CITIZENS BANK

I O Won't · CITIZENS BANK

Iowa 42
Penn State 35
(OT)

PSU Dots The "I" In Win · CITIZENS BANK

at Ohio State 13
Penn State 7

Penn State 61
Michigan State 7

Spartans Are History · CITIZENS BANK

CAPITAL ONE BOWL, JANUARY 1, 2003
Lions Win Catfight! · CITIZENS BANK · Orlando, Florida

Auburn 13
Penn State 9
(Capital One Bowl)

2003

Season Record:
Won 3, Lost 9;
in Big Ten: 1–7, 9th

Final Rankings:
Not Ranked

Penn State 23
Temple 10

Ohio State 21
Penn State 20

Minnesota 20
Penn State 14

Boston College 27
Penn State 14

at Northwestern 17
Penn State 7

Wisconsin 30
Penn State 23

at Nebraska 18
Penn State 10

Penn State 52
Indiana 7

at Purdue 28
Penn State 14

Penn State 32
Kent State 10

at Michigan State 41
Penn State 10

at Iowa 26
Penn State 14

Crush the Orange

1972 Variation
Original appeared
without bank logo.

Pulverize the Panthers

2001 Variation
Original used Mellon
Bank logo.

1972 Variation
Original appeared
without bank logo.

Nuttin' Doin', Buckeyes
'01
CITIZENS BANK

Trip the Terrapins

1972 Variation
Original appeared
without bank logo.

Pulverize the Panthers

2001 Variation
Original used Mellon
Bank logo.

1972 Variation
Metal back substituted
for green cardboard.

Miss-ery
'01
CITIZENS BANK

Wallop the Wolfpack

1972 Variation
Original appeared
without bank logo.

BACK
THE LIONS

1973 Variation
Original appeared
with bank logo.

2001 Variation
Original used Mellon
Bank logo.

Hoosier Kidding
'01
CITIZENS BANK

Wallop the Wolfpack

1972 Variation
Metal back substituted
for green cardboard.

central counties bank says
Skin the Bears

1974 Variation
Original appeared with
white background.

175

BACK THE LIONS

1973
First 12–0
season

**WE'RE NUMBER 1
PENN STATE
central counties bank**

1978
First No. 1
ranking under
Joe Paterno

**central counties bank says
First at the Gate
in '78!**

1978
First game
in expanded
Beaver Stadium

1980
125 years since
Penn State's
founding in 1855

**central counties bank says
HAPPY
125th
PENN
STATE**

1982
First national
championship

**central counties bank salutes
NITTANY
LIONS
#1
National Champions 1982**

ABOUT THE AUTHORS

Martin Ford was born and raised in the shadow of Beaver Stadium in Lemont, Pennsylvania. He graduated from Penn State in 1975 with a degree from the College of Human Development, where he and his soon-to-be wife Sheri Coughlin enjoyed taking classes from outstanding faculty like assistant professor (and later Penn State president) Graham Spanier. If Martin had known what the Golden Gophers would do to the Nittany Lions in 1999, he perhaps would not have left for Minnesota to seek a PhD in child psychology there. However, that did enable him to follow in his father's footsteps and become a professor—at Stanford University's School of Education, where he created motivational systems theory using his father's living systems framework. In 1993 he and Sheri left California with their two sons so Martin could seek a position in closer proximity to Beaver Stadium. He found a perfect match in northern Virginia at the College of Education and Human Development at George Mason University, the largest academic institution in the country without a football team. Since then he has combined scholarly research and writing on human

motivation with the quest for perfect slogans for the game-day football buttons.

Russell Ford was born in Kansas, but was brought to a new home at the base of Mount Nittany by his parents, Don and Carol, at the beginning of his dad's tenure on the Penn State faculty. His brothers, Martin, Doug, and Cam, soon arrived on the scene, and collectively the "Ford boys" set their sights on attending the great university just over the hill. Russell graduated from Penn State in 1973 with dual degrees in park and

recreation administration and community development, which he received at a Beaver Stadium commencement from the dean of his college, who also just happened to be his dad. Coincidentally, his graduation speaker was Joe Paterno. After graduation Russ spent summers working for the U.S. Forest Service, but in between he came out of the woods to earn a graduate degree in city and regional planning from the University of North Carolina at Chapel Hill. He took those skills to Harrisburg, Pennsylvania, where he became a leader in revitalizing Pennsylvania's capital city through development of office, retail, residential, hotel, cultural arts, and public facility projects. Today he is the president and CEO of one of the largest economic development corporations in Pennsylvania, and fortunately for this book, he is also a top expert on the Penn State football buttons. He and his wife, Penn State alum Barbara Guthrie of State College, take great pride in watching their three sons and two daughters continue the Ford family tradition as Penn State students and graduates.